HOW TO BUY A
HOUSE

HOW TO BUY A
HOUSE

Practical Advice Based
on Interviews with
Actual Home Buyers

Cyrus A. Yoakam

Stackpole Books

Copyright © 1988 by Stackpole Books

Published by
STACKPOLE BOOKS
Cameron and Kelker Streets
P.O. Box 1831
Harrisburg, PA 17105

All rights reserved, including the right to reproduce this book or portions thereof in any form or by any means, electronic or mechanical, including photocopying, recording, or by any information storage and retrieval system, without permission in writing from the publisher. All inquiries should be addressed to Stackpole Books, Cameron and Kelker Streets, P.O. Box 1831, Harrisburg, Pennsylvania 17105.

Printed in the United States of America

10 9 8 7 6 5 4 3 2 1

Library of Congress Cataloging-in-Publication Data

Yoakam, Cyrus A.
   How to buy a house: practical advice based on interviews with actual home buyers / Cyrus A. Yoakam.
     p.   cm.
   Includes index.
   ISBN 0-8117-2252-X : $9.95
   1. House buying. I. Title.
HD1379.Y63   1988
643'.12—dc19
                                              88-12236
                                                  CIP

Contents

1 SEARCH PREPARATION

Initial Steps	16
Financial (and Other) Preparations	21
Home Price and Value	26
Using a Lawyer	27

2 SEARCH STRATEGIES

Timing and Location	34
Buyer's Agent	39
Motivated Sellers	43
For Sale by Owner	45
Foreclosures	47
The Multilist	49
Miscellaneous Strategies	52
Long-Distance Hunting	55

3 CHOOSING AN AGENT

Agents and Agencies	59
Locating a Good Agent	62
Screening an Agent	64

4 WORKING WITH THE AGENT

Meeting with the Agent	71
Preparing to Visit Homes	73
Inspecting Houses with the Agent	77
Ethics and the Agent	82

5 LOOKING AT HOMES

Before Arriving	88
Top Inspection Priorities	89
Checking the Rest	92

6 THE OFFER

Preparing to Make the Offer	101
Making the Offer	107
Delivering the Offer	111

7 DOCUMENTS OF SALE

The Binder and Earnest Money	124
The Sales Contract	128
The Deed	139

8 FINANCING THE SALE

Finding a Mortgage	144
Selecting the Right Mortgage	146
The Down Payment	155
Applying for the Mortgage Loan	158
Processing the Loan	164
The Appraisal	167
Mortgage Insurance	170
Amortization and Equity	172

9 SAFEGUARDING YOUR INVESTMENT

The Building Inspection	174
Pest Inspection	180
Radon Testing	183
Home Warranties	185
Title Search and Insurance	189
Homeowners' Insurance	193
Property (and Other) Taxes	197

10 THE CLOSING

Preparing for Closing	200
Closing Day	205

Illustrations

Comparables File	20
Classified Ad	21
Loan Shopping List	22
Buying a House: Summary of Costs	24
Sample Lawyer–Client Memo	32
Sample Buyer's Agent Contract	42
Sample Multiple Listing	51
Home Inspection Worksheet	94
Sample Counteroffer	117
Sample Binder	125
Sample Sales Contract	132
The Mortgage Trail	147
Sample Gift Letter	157

Acknowledgments

Many people helped in the research and writing of this book. My thanks to all.

I'm especially grateful to M. David Detweiler, president of Stackpole Books, who conceived the idea for this book and kept me on course; to Sally Atwater and Patricia Hazur, who edited the manuscript; to Tracy Patterson, who designed the book; and to Mimi Lambert, Director of Education, Greater Harrisburg Board of Realtors, and Linda Lloyd, Director, Real Estate Institute of Pennsylvania, who spent hours answering my questions.

I'm also grateful to the twenty-four recent home buyers who were interviewed for this book. They represent all income levels, and bought homes in rural, suburban, and inner-city locations, and in small and large metropolitan areas. Their detailed accounts of their experiences were an immense help.

Introduction

Buying a house is a big job. It can be intimidating, frustrating, and expensive. The goal of this book is to familiarize you with the home-buying process, making you more comfortable and knowledgeable, and thereby a more effective buyer.

Home buyers find three areas of trouble: preparing for the hunt, finding and working with a good agent, and negotiating the deal. In this book you'll learn how to deal with these trouble areas, and others, by going through the entire process of home buying, beginning with the first step and ending as you finish the closing.

Most books on home buying have page after page of *whats*: what types of mortgages are available, what to look at in houses, what costs are involved. In this book, however, a question-and-answer format stresses the *hows* of home buying. This book will tell you how to find an agent, how to get a building inspection, how to arrange financing. You'll learn what works, what's a waste of time; when you can be assertive, when you can't; when something's done because it's legal, or because it's just customary.

This is not, however, a do-it-yourself book. You'll still need professional help along the way; this book will tell you how and when to seek it. But by reading this book and following the steps, you'll be prepared for the tasks of house inspecting, negotiating, making financial arrangements, and, finally, protecting your carefully acquired investment.

1

Search Preparation

Buying a house without being prepared is like taking an exam without any study. Only the stakes are much higher.

In this chapter you will wade right into the real estate world, getting acquainted with the market and the tools of house hunting. Why inspect a dozen houses only to find that you can't afford any of them? Why wait until you make an offer on a house to learn about sales contracts?

You will start out house hunting with a sense of adventure and high hopes. But without preparation, you may feel, as one buyer put it, "dragged along and never quite in control."

INITIAL STEPS

What are the initial steps?

First, list your needs and wants. Ask yourself what is motivating you to consider buying a house.

Your *needs* are what you *must* have in a house—location, financing, move-in date, and so on. Your *wants* are what it would be nice to have. You will stick with your basic needs throughout house hunting; your wants may change as your search continues. So may your expectations.

Here are two examples of a needs–wants list:

The Smiths	**The Joneses**
Needs:	*Needs:*
four bedrooms	two bedrooms plus office space
Hillsboro school district	within thirty minutes of downtown
$65,000, tops	low maintenance
down payment less than $5,000	move in by June 30
Wants:	*Wants:*
large yard	fireplace
seller financing	full basement
schools within walking distance	wooded lot

"We had to lower our expectations, and deal with the frustration of not finding the 'perfect house.' That was our most important lesson."
—E.F.

Second, figure out what price you can afford.

Start with two rules of thumb, which serve as guidelines to establish an upper limit for your spending:

- Your monthly mortgage and property tax payments should not exceed 28 percent of your monthly gross income, to allow adequate income for the remainder of your expenses.

- You can afford a house priced at roughly two times your gross annual income(s).

But you have to live within a budget. Let's see how loans of $50,000 and $100,000 translate into monthly mortgage payments at three interest rates:

	Interest	Monthly Mortgage Payment
$50,000 loan (30 years) at	12%	$514
	10	439
	8	367
$100,000 loan (30 years) at	12%	$1,029
	10	878
	8	734

On top of this, you will probably need a down payment of 5 to 20 percent of your purchase price. For a $50,000 home that means $2,500 to $10,000 down; for a $100,000 home, $5,000 to $20,000.

"Many people who contact me have virtually no savings—and no idea of the up-front costs (down payment, closing costs). They shouldn't even be looking."—J.V., agent

"I considered not only what I could afford, but also my priorities. One was travel. I wanted to stay well below the rule-of-thumb guidelines, so I could maintain a large travel budget."—W.H.

Now, get an overview of the housing market. You can accomplish this in a day or two, using the following steps:

- Drop in on three or four real estate offices. Don't make an appointment; there is usually someone on duty. Experience talking to a real estate agent. The agent will try to snare you as his client. Stay loose a little longer.
- Look through newspaper ads. They will probably be separated into homes sold through agents and homes sold directly by owners.
- Call your local For Sale By Owner office, listed in the Yellow Pages, to see what's available in its listings.
- If you are new to the territory, drive around.

How do I learn more?

Become adept at using the tools of the market. The three most important tools: the multilist, the comparables file, and the classified ads.

"This was our first house-hunting experience. We started out with a ceiling of $100,000. Prices were rising daily. In order to get what we wanted, we ended up paying $220,000."—F.M.

"I wanted something close to downtown. To get a feel for nearby older areas, my fiancée and I went on several Candlelight Tours of the city's historic district. After a few, we got concerned about the maintenance on these old homes. So

SEARCH PREPARATION

we began to look for new developments in these same areas."—W.H.

What is a multilist?

This is your most important tool. It is a listing, in book form, of all the houses for sale by participating real estate agencies in the area.

What information does a multilist contain?

Most entries contain a picture of the house. All include a description of the house and lot, information on utilities, taxes, school district, financing, and reason for selling, plus the names and phone numbers of the listing agents and sellers.

By studying the entries, you can save time on calling listing agents with questions, or driving around to see what a house looks like.

What is a comparables file?

It is a listing of recently sold homes, presented by street or neighborhood. It tells the address, type of house, list price, purchase price, and sometimes the age. After reviewing it, you will have a good idea of what you can expect to pay for the type of house you want in a particular area. Virtually all real estate offices maintain such files. At some offices it may simply be the quarterly report of sales from the area multilist service. Scan the pages of the neighborhoods that interest you, and ask your agent for copies of the relevant pages.

Comparables File

Main Street		List	Sold For
120 Main	3BR 2-story	$63,900	$60,000
315 Main	2BR duplex	49,500	45,200
327 Main	3BR ranch	68,500	62,750
544 Main	4BR cape cod	75,900	71,400
769 Main	3BR ranch	59,900	55,000

Note the difference between the list price and the purchase price. These homes sold for 5% to 10% less than the owners hoped to get.

How do I read between the lines in the classifieds?

Be a skeptic.

- Look for what the ads don't say. If no location is listed, it's probably a bad location.

- Assume that the good things not mentioned in the ad don't exist. No mention of basement? There may be just a crawl space. No glowing accounts of trees and shrubs? It's probably pretty barren.

- Does the ad give a grudging disclosure of a tiny defect, or read "needs cosmetic work"? Get out your tool chest, or maybe a bulldozer.

However, an ad has to stick to something bordering on the truth. If it says there are a basement and two bathrooms, they exist.

SEARCH PREPARATION

Classified Ad

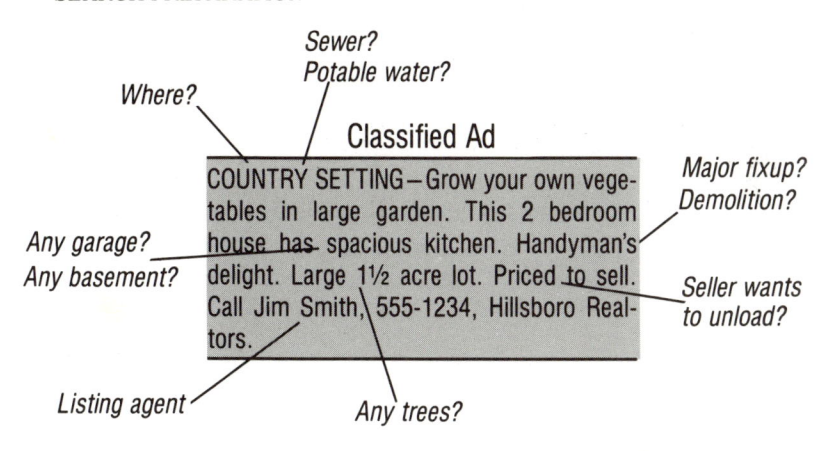

Where? —
Sewer? Potable water? —
Any garage? Any basement? —
Listing agent —
Any trees? —
Major fixup? Demolition? —
Seller wants to unload? —

> COUNTRY SETTING—Grow your own vegetables in large garden. This 2 bedroom house has spacious kitchen. Handyman's delight. Large 1½ acre lot. Priced to sell. Call Jim Smith, 555-1234, Hillsboro Realtors.

FINANCIAL (AND OTHER) PREPARATIONS

How can I find out what types of mortgages are available?

Shop around. Look in your Sunday paper for a list of mortgages available in your area. Call a couple lenders that look good, basing your choices on your needs list. Ask for more details on their terms. Start a "Loan Shopping List" to compare one lender with another. Also, ask one of the agents you've met to do a computer run on mortgages available, including government-insured mortgages.

How do I "get qualified"?

Call the mortgage department of the bank, credit union, or savings and loan that looked best on your loan shopping list. Ask for a fifteen-minute appoint-

Loan Shopping List

Lender	Contact Person	Rate	Points	Fees	Lock-in	If Adjustable Rate Life Cap	If Adjustable Rate Periodic Cap
Hills Mort.	Ted	8.0%	5	$300	45 days	5%	2%
Hills Bank	Jan	8.2%	3	$200	60 days	6%	1%
Hills S&L	Bud	10.4%	1	$250	60 days	—	—
Jones Bank	Ed	10.6%	1	$300	60 days		
Jones S&L	Sue	10.1%	3	$250			
Jones Mort.	Tom						
Peoples Bank							

ment to get qualified for buying a house. Then take along a list of your income, assets, and debts. While there, ask the loan officer to give you conditional or spot approval for a mortgage.

What is conditional mortgage approval?

This is a process similar to the actual approval of a home loan, except that you do not have a sales contract in hand. What you get is a written statement saying that the lending institution has approved a certain number of dollars for a home loan. In negotiations, this will carry more weight with the seller than a qualifying form that merely says you can shop in a certain price range.

The lender will probably charge you for the credit check involved in conditional approval. But the cost may be only half the $150 to $200 you would pay for an actual mortgage approval.

SEARCH PREPARATION

What if I don't qualify for the type or price of house I want?

If you have your heart set on a certain type of house and don't qualify, you might try alternative financing. Here are a couple of examples:

- Ask your parents (or an investment-minded friend) to make your down payment, and put their names on the title along with yours. That way, your combined incomes will be used in the qualifying process.

- Your parents (or friend) buy the house you want. Then they lease it to you. You make the monthly mortgage payments, with perhaps a subsidy from them until you get a boost in income.

"In order to get money for a down payment, I asked my parents. They agreed and, at the lender's request, put their house up as collateral."—J.W.

Should I sell my house before buying another?

Yes. But don't sell it so fast that you have to rent until you find another. Use a cautious approach:

- List your place for sale, and then start house hunting.

- If you find a buyer, make sure your contract states that you will sell only if you find an-

23

Buying a House: Summary of Costs

Mortgage

Conditional mortgage approval	$75–$150
Application fee	$150–$300
Origination fee (points)	1–4% of loan
Appraisal	$125–$250
Mortgage insurance	Varies with buyer's age and price of house.

Inspections/Protection

Building inspection	$100–$350
Pest inspection	$35–$100
Radon inspection	$0–$150
Home warranty: new home	$3–5 per $1,000 house price, minimum $200
used home	$300–$400
Title search and insurance	$200–$1,000 depending on house price
Homeowners' insurance	$2–4 per $1,000 price

Closing

Survey of property	$100–$200
Recording deed/mortgage	$20–$40
Transfer taxes	1% of price or a flat fee

Buyer's Agent (optional) 3–7% of price

---

other house within a certain time, say, ninety days.

- If you find the house you want to buy, write an offer that says you will buy only if you sell your present house.

Real estate agents and lawyers are experienced in making these types of sales dovetail. They do it often.

SEARCH PREPARATION

Should I learn about sales contracts now?

Yes. You will use this instrument when you get to the crucial negotiating stage. Get familiar with it now. Pick up a copy for a dollar or two at a well-stocked office supply store, or ask an agent or mortgage officer for one.

Then make a practice run. Pretend you are making an offer on that dream house in your needs and wants list—one you can afford.

Start with the terms of your conditional mortgage: amount, down payment, interest rate, and number of years. Then add the conditions of sale, such as a building inspection and an occupancy date. If you have run across an especially helpful agent or mortgage officer by now, ask one of them to review your trial run.

Are there certain emotional stages in hunting for a house?

Yes. Especially if this is your first home-buying experience.

During the first six to eight houses, your mind will be "sampling the market." You may resist making an offer, even if a house is just right for you. For the next six to eight houses, you will feel more confident about the market, and be more likely to make an offer. Or you may return to an earlier house, and make an offer on it.

If you have seen fifteen homes, and have rejected all, a sense of bewilderment may set in. At this point your agent, if you have one, may ask you to review your needs and wants—or even your motives for house hunting. A very good idea.

"A buyer will sometimes want to return to the first house, only to find it sold. He will tell me [his agent] that it was just the one he wanted. I will already know that. But to have suggested that he make an offer on the first house he sees would seem pushy to him. So I refrain from such suggestions early in the game."—M.L., agent

What other sources might I use to help me in buying a house?

Consult *The New York Times Guide to Buying or Building a Home,* by William Connolly, second edition, 1984 (Times Books, $16.95 plus postage).

HOME PRICE AND VALUE

What goes into the price and value of a house?

Home prices and bargains are not such a mystery if you know the five components of real estate value. Price is just one. Don't overlook the other four.

- Location
- Property condition
- Financing
- Seller's motivation and flexibility
- Price

} = Housing Value

SEARCH PREPARATION

What can I expect to pay for a house?

The average new house in the U.S. costs over $100,000, and the average used house is approaching six figures, according to the National Association of Realtors (NAR).

Prices are highest in the suburbs of large metropolitan areas (over two million people) and in the Northeast. They are lowest in old center cities, the Midwest, and rural areas. The average home in the New York City area costs *twice* as much as one in the Chicago area. Likewise, the average Chicago home costs nearly twice the average Decatur (Illinois) house, only 150 miles away.

What are the trends in home prices?

Prices are going up. By the year 2000, they will be double what they were in the mid-1980s, according to the NAR. However, personal income is also expected to double. So a house will still take about the same chunk out of your budget.

USING A LAWYER

Why would I need a lawyer?

A lawyer represents *you*, not the seller. This is especially important when drawing up legal contracts.

"In New York, you get a lawyer first, then a real estate agent. In Central Pennsylvania, it seems that few buyers use lawyers. Maybe it's the

folkways here; maybe the laws are less complicated. Perhaps there is more trust."—C.F.

Should I use my lender's or agent's agency lawyer?

Not if you want someone to represent you 100 percent.

It may be tempting to use the agency lawyer to draw up or review contracts. After all, he or she is handy, and often cheap or even free. Be particularly wary of using a lender's lawyer. He represents the lender, who wants the loan on his terms—not necessarily yours. Finally, never use the same lawyer the seller is using.

What duties can my lawyer perform?

In a real estate transaction, the lawyer's duties fall into four categories:

- Drawing up or reviewing contracts (offer, sales contract, mortgage). This is the most common duty.
- Negotiating on your behalf.
- Advising on inspections and other closing procedures.
- Sitting in on the closing.

Some buyers feel perfectly comfortable having their agent handle these duties. But many hire a lawyer to at least review contracts, a move you should seriously consider.

SEARCH PREPARATION

When should I hire a lawyer?

Before you actively begin house hunting.
This way you have one available any time you need legal advice during the search. Don't wait until after you've made an offer; then it may be too late.

Will my agent object?

Some won't be too happy. They may insist that they know the legal ropes, or can call on the agency lawyer for advice. But remember, your agent and his agency technically represent the seller.

How do I find a good real estate lawyer?

Ask for recommendations from an appraiser, bank mortgage officer, or friends who have recently bought a house. Most pros in the field will recommend a lawyer more readily than they will suggest a real estate agent. Another source is the *Martindale-Hubbell Law Directory.* Consult it after getting a few recommendations. Available in most good reference libraries, the directory is organized by geographic area. It lists many, though hardly all, of the lawyers in the United States.

The directory lists the birth date, college and law school, degrees earned, year law practice began, membership in the American Bar Association, and name of law firm. It also rates many lawyers on diligence, reliability, and ethics, and on legal ability. The ratings, done by peers, give you some indication of quality. However, they may overlook or underrate some promising and diligent newcomers.

How should I contact the recommended lawyer?

Phone him. Ask about his fees and residential real estate experience.

Local custom dictates a lot of the real estate business. So be sure he didn't just arrive in town. If you have special problems (like a for-sale-by-owner deal, or a large land purchase), ask whether he has handled such cases.

As you talk, get a sense of whether you would feel comfortable asking this person questions during your home buying. You may be asking a lot of questions. After selecting a lawyer by phone, arrange to meet with him to discuss your case, and nail down the exact fees.

"I was concerned about the seller's proposal for two deeds. So I used that as a screening question when I called each lawyer. The first three I phoned only offered suggestions for making the two-deed arrangement less damaging to me. But the fourth lawyer I called explained why the two-deed arrangement was poor. He said he would try to get rid of it if hired. I hired him."
—J.H.

How are the lawyer's fees set?

Flat fee. This is probably the most common, and usually the best for you. You know ahead of time what the cost will be and what he will do. Usually in the $250 to $750 range.

The lawyer may say that legal work above the "nor-

SEARCH PREPARATION

mal work" will be charged by the hour. This is fine, as long as you and he agree on what is expected for the flat fee.

Hourly fee. Okay if the lawyer can give you an idea of how many hours will be involved. Most buyers using a lawyer require from five to fifteen hours and pay $50 to $150 per hour. However, one buyer in a for-sale-by-owner deal needed his lawyer for twenty-five hours. Fortunately for him, the lawyer charged a flat fee.

Percentage of purchase price fee. One percent of purchase price is common, but beware of lawyers who want to charge you on this basis. Usually it takes no more time to handle a $100,000 deal than it does a $50,000 deal.

When do I pay?

If you are charged a flat fee, you may pay 15 to 20 percent of the fee, the "retainer," at the outset. Then you pay the balance at the closing. This is reasonable. Don't, however, pay the entire amount at the beginning.

The same procedure, retainer first and balance at closing, also applies to the hourly and percentage methods of payment. Some lawyers do not require any payment until the work is completed.

Do I sign a contract with my lawyer?

You can, but it is not necessary. Write down the duties and payments that you and the lawyer have agreed to. Have him initial a copy and the original, and give him the copy.

Sample Lawyer–Client Memo

Lawyer Fee
For legal assistance in closing residential real estate deal.

Includes:
- Reviewing the contract and related documents
- Giving advice
- Helping make changes, if not major negotiations
- Sitting in on settlement
- Title search

$315–325 without Title Insurance
    $382 with Title Insurance

Additional charges of $75 per hour for services above and beyond the normal course of negotiating such a contract. The client, John and Jane Doe, would be consulted in advance.

Confirmed by Hilda Hill of Hill, Hill, and Hill on the phone on [date].

Initials: _____

> Clients:
> John and Jane Doe
> 1234 Hill St.
> Hillsboro, USA 00000
> (000) 555-5555

2

Search Strategies

You now have an idea of what you need and can afford in a house. You know what the market is like. In this chapter you will learn how and when to go after the house you want.

The strategies you use depend on your circumstances. Let's suppose that you can't afford much, but location is not important. You also have some time to look. This situation allows you to use several strategies, including hunting in the "off-season" and seeking out foreclosures, motivated sellers, and for-sale-by-owner houses.

On the other hand, suppose that you have a substantial income. It is June—the height of the season— and you are moving to another city where the market is tight. You'll need plenty of help in your new town and ways to explore the market fast. This is where you might benefit by hiring a buyer's agent and learning ways to gain an edge on other buyers.

By the end of this chapter, with search preparation and strategies under your belt, you will be ready for the hunt, whatever your circumstances.

TIMING AND LOCATION

How much time should I allow to buy a house?

At least five months: two months to find one, and three more to obtain financing and close the deal.

After you have spelled out your needs and wants to an agent, he can give you a better estimate of time needed. If possible, build in an extra month at the beginning. During this month, prepare for the search and hunt at a leisurely pace, without the pressure of deadlines.

Does house-hunting strategy depend on my deadline?

With a tight deadline, you maintain a vigil on the latest multilists, hot sheets, and sales rumors. You rely on one agent for efficiency.

Without a deadline, you use the same tools, but you can drive around more, chat with people in target neighborhoods, use listing agents, and revisit houses.

SEARCH STRATEGIES

How do I begin?

Resist the temptation to do things helter-skelter.

- Don't begin by inspecting for-sale-by-owner homes. Develop an eye for inspecting by first going with an agent.
- Don't call agents asking for drive-by addresses. You can get these in the multilist.
- Don't make an appointment with an agent to inspect just one house.
- Don't drive several miles to view a model home, unless you know that the contractor builds homes in your desired location.
- Don't take others with you to inspect houses. This includes kids, dogs, parents, and well-meaning friends.

How long does the average home stay on the market?

Nationwide, two to three months.

However, in fast-growing areas, homes are snapped up in two weeks or less. In cities with sluggish economies, houses are for sale five months or more. Homes remain on sale longer in winter in the snow belt. In the South, the variation among seasons is less pronounced.

When should I look for a house?

House hunting is most enjoyable in mild, sunny weather. However, you live in a house during all four seasons. Look at houses during the worst times: dead of winter, rush hours, hot days, rainy days, dark evenings. Also look on weekends, when the neighbors are out in the yards and the kids are noisy. Such factors can tip your decision.

"It came down to two houses, one old and one new. My wife visited both on a hot June day. First, she looked at the older house. The second floor was hot; the third floor, unbearable. The new house was cool all around. We bought the new house."—C.F.

"After we signed the contract, I wanted to visit the house in the rain to check for leaks in the roof or water in the basement. One rainy day, we called the sellers and asked to come out. They said it was not convenient. Any other days, which were sunny, were fine with them. That should have tipped us off that there was a problem with leaks."—D.G.

What time of year are most houses for sale?

Spring and early summer.

Many people being transferred in the summer put their houses up for sale as early as January. They need time to sell the old place before buying in a new location. So even midwinter may bring decent offerings.

But be careful about midwinter prices. Owners putting their homes up for sale in early January may be

SEARCH STRATEGIES

testing the waters. If by April they haven't had any nibbles, they may reduce their price.

When are houses the cheapest?

Late fall and winter. The seller either has had the house on the market a long time, or is selling in a hurry. He is willing to negotiate.

A change of seasons can turn potential buyers away, making less competition for you. A neighborhood that looks like a bustling Camelot in summer can seem like the deserted Badlands by late fall.

"The neighborhood didn't look too presentable. The lake was drained for about eight weeks that fall. Three or four visitors seemed semi-interested in the house we were renting. However, apparently no one made an offer."
—C.C.

How important is the location?

Your list of needs and wants will give you the answer.

For some, location is the number-one need. For others, it is not critical.

"Our daughter was beginning high school. We needed to remain in the same school district. We had a nucleus of friends in that area, and I liked the quiet of the suburban setting. As avid swimmers, we wanted to remain near the pools where we swim year-round. Yes, location was critical for us."—J.H.

37

"Though I had lived and worked in Camp Hill for several years, we were not committed to any one area. We began by traveling through several areas with our agent, spending one day each in Mechanicsburg, Carlisle, uptown Harrisburg, and so on. We ended up in Harrisburg, but only because that was where we found a house we liked."—B.C.

How can I learn about a neighborhood I'm interested in?

Talk to people. Find out what they are like. Learn about community activities.

"We found neighborhoods that we liked, even where no houses were for sale. We talked to people out in their yards, found out what they were like. We spread the word that we were looking in the area."—E.F.

Should I hire someone to help me house hunt?

Real estate agents technically represent the sellers. Therefore, you might benefit from hiring your own agent, often called a buyer's agent. However, such agents are rare, and might not be available in your area.

BUYER'S AGENT

What is a buyer's agent?

This is a real estate agent hired to represent you, and you alone. The rationale is to give you (the buyer) and the seller equal representation.

What services does he perform for me?

He can help you with any and all phases of home buying:

Market research

- Checking ads and multilistings.
- Obtaining comparables.
- Researching the future of the town or neighborhood (land use plans, economic development, highway construction).

Inspections

- Doing preliminary inspections without you, to weed out unsuitable homes.
- Going with you to inspect houses.

Negotiations

- Lowering the purchase price.
- Hammering out the conditions of the sales contract.

Service after the contract

- Arranging financing.
- Obtaining professional inspections.
- Helping you prepare for closing.
- Attending closing.

With these services in mind, you can use him in one of three ways:

- Use his services during each step, as adviser and leg-man. He screens and suggests, you make the decisions. This is the most common way to employ a buyer's agent.

- Have him handle certain matters that you are too busy for or uncomfortable with, such as prescreening homes or advising on purchase price. If you are well prepared for the hunt, you should need the buyer's agent only for certain jobs, such as negotiations. This is cheaper than using him at every step.

- Hand over the entire job to him, and say, "See you at the closing." This is going overboard in most cases. You should at least inspect the houses, negotiate the purchase, and select the loan with your agent.

Whichever route you choose, be sure your needs and wants are being met.

Are buyer's agents effective?

Yes, they can be, especially where housing is tight and bidding wars are possible.

SEARCH STRATEGIES

Hire one if any of the following conditions apply:

- You want a special, hard-to-find house.
- You are hunting long distance.
- You are in a hurry.
- The market is tight, and houses are snapped up in a week.
- You are buying a for-sale-by-owner house.
- You are a first-time home buyer.

How much does a buyer's agent cost?

A rough rule of thumb is about 5 percent of purchase price, or $5,000 on a $100,000 house.

Charges are made by flat fee, hourly rate, or percentage of your purchase price. The percentage method is the most common. If you use the agent primarily to find you a good house, the charge is about 3 to 4 percent of purchase price. If you add on negotiations and postcontract duties, the fee may go as high as 7 percent.

The buyer's agent will contend that through his house-screening and negotiation skills, he can save you that amount or more in the purchase price.

What should I include in a contract with a buyer's agent?

The contract should contain the following items:

- Your name and his.

- Date the contract begins and ends, usually for three to six months.
- Services to be provided.
- Agent's fee.
- Right to terminate the contract on ten to thirty days' notice if you are not satisfied.
- Clause saying, "If I don't buy, I don't pay."

Sample Buyer's Agent Contract

Agreement:
I _____ agree to retain _____
　　　　(buyer)　　　　　　　　　　　　　　　　　(agent)
for the purpose of exclusively assisting me to locate a property of a nature outlined below. The agreement will terminate on _____ .
　　(date)

Property Requirements:
Nature:
Location:
Price and Condition:

Fee. The buyer agrees to pay the buyer's agent a nonrefundable fee of $ _____ for initial consultation and research, and $ _____ or _____% of purchase price for obtaining a suitable property.

Agent's obligations. The agent will use diligence in locating a property acceptable to the client, and in negotiating terms of purchase. He will act for the client only, and will not accept a fee from the seller.

Signed: _____ date
　　　　　　_____ agent
　　　　　　_____ client (buyer)

SEARCH STRATEGIES

How do I locate a buyer's agent?

Buyer's agents work mostly in large cities. The organization Who's Who in Creative Real Estate, P.O. Box 23275, Ventura, CA, publishes a directory listing about 400 buyer's agents in the U.S. These agents have attended courses on being a buyer's agent and have conducted at least one transaction. The directory costs $25 and is not generally available in libraries.

Many others, not listed in the directory, work as buyer's agents. You can locate them in the Yellow Pages under Real Estate, or by calling your local Board of Realtors.

Can I hire a local real estate agent as my buyer's agent?

Yes. Since real estate agents are self-employed, you can hire one as your representative—for a fee, of course.

Until recently, the National Association of Realtors opposed the concept of the buyer's agent. Now they support it, and traditional real estate agents are becoming more receptive to this new role.

MOTIVATED SELLERS

What types of sellers are there?

Many. For your purposes, you want to know how to spot them—and how highly motivated they are to meet your terms.

Some sellers want to deal right now and will give you a bargain. Others don't mind dragging their feet for months until they get their price and terms. For the real estate investor, finding highly motivated sellers is perhaps his key strategy.

What can I gain by finding a motivated seller?

The leverage to negotiate the terms *you* want. This includes not only purchase price but also who pays the closing costs, when you can close and move in, and perhaps even financing by the seller.

Who might be a motivated seller?

Most sellers are highly motivated to sell, not because their property is bad, but because of personal problems or considerations.

Investor Robert Allen has come up with twenty reasons people become motivated sellers. Thirteen are personal. Only two have to do with the property itself. Here are the ones you will encounter most often:

Personal	**Property**
Divorce	Obsolescence
Job transfer	Poor location
Death	
Retirement	
Out-of-town owners	
Debts	
Inability to maintain	
Sickness	

How do I detect these motivated sellers?

Look for clues in the multilist, and in the answers and actions of the seller.

First, the multilist will tell you the reason the seller is selling. The reason listed is sometimes specific (retirement), sometimes vague (buying another house).

Second, while visiting a house, ask the seller how long the house has been for sale, when he must move, and specifically why he is moving. If he says it's been on sale six months, or he must move next week, or he's being transferred, you are probably dealing with a motivated seller. If you feel uncomfortable asking these questions, or if the seller is not home, your agent can find out the answers.

Third, notice whether the seller is going all out to facilitate the sale. For example, is the place immaculate? Does he hand you a prepared sheet of information about the house? These usually indicate a highly motivated seller, but they may also just be signs of good marketing.

If the seller is motivated, what should I do?

Make your offer considerably below what comparable houses are selling for, as much as 25 percent below.

FOR SALE BY OWNER

What is a for-sale-by-owner arrangement?

The seller markets the house without the help of a

listing agent. The arrangement is known by the letters FSBO.

Why would a seller try to sell the house by himself?

For one of two reasons: to save money, or to avoid inspections and appraisals.

A listing agent costs the seller about 6 percent of the purchase price in commission. A FSBO house is a good deal for you *if* the seller passes the savings along.

But if the seller is going the FSBO route to avoid inspections or appraisals, watch out! The house may have certain defects that would cause a lender to reject your loan application, or a government building inspector to cite code violations.

Are there many for-sale-by-owner houses?

No. Perhaps 5 to 15 percent of the houses on the market in any given area. Many FSBO sellers fail to find a buyer on their own and eventually hire a listing agent.

How do I find for-sale-by-owner homes?

Your primary source is the classified ads in the newspaper. In some areas, there are also For-Sale-by-Owner agencies. They list these FSBO houses for a fee (to the seller) but do not show the homes. You can call or go to their offices to check the listings. Finally, a few sellers don't even take out an ad. They just stick a For Sale sign in front of their house.

What can I gain by dealing directly with the seller?

You might get a bargain if the seller sets a realistic price, and if he knocks off about 6 percent for the sales commission. That's two *ifs*. You and the seller act as your own agents, so neither of you pays a commission.

In addition, you might find the seller willing to finance the sale. Then you don't have to worry about qualifying for a bank loan.

Are there any pitfalls?

You are negotiating without the benefit of a buffer, the agent. Depending on your personalities, this could be a little nerve-wracking. Second, you don't have an agent to guide you through the intricacies of obtaining financing and closing the deal. Hiring a lawyer to represent you is a must.

The buyers of FSBO houses believe they have gotten good prices. And by using lawyers in the contractual stages, they feel adequately represented.

FORECLOSURES

What is a foreclosure?

A foreclosure is a legal proceeding in which the lender or a government agency takes over ownership of a house, because the owner has failed to meet his mortgage or tax payments.

How many houses for sale are foreclosures?

Not a large number. But during a sick economy, foreclosures are worth investigating.

Can I save much by buying a foreclosed house?

Sometimes. If the seller fixes up the foreclosed houses before marketing them, they may list only a little below market value. In other cases, where the lender or government agency doesn't want to bother, you can save 20 or 25 percent.

How do I find out about foreclosures?

From newspaper ads, mortgage officers of lending institutions, and the Federal National Mortgage Association (Washington, D.C.).

How do I make an offer on a foreclosure?

Some foreclosed homes are put up for sale at public auctions. For others, you make an offer to the lending institution.

Could I encounter any problems with a foreclosed house?

Yes. Often you will buy the house as is. No fixing up by the seller, no warranties.

Most states have laws giving the prior owner the "right of redemption." Under this right, the previous

SEARCH STRATEGIES

owner can buy back the house for a certain period of time, say, six months. During this period, you do not take title to the house or move in. If, at the end of the redemption period, the previous owner has not made up his payments, then you take title.

THE MULTILIST

Are multilists available in all parts of the country?

Yes, except in some rural areas. All urban areas have a multiple listing service.

How many houses are on the multilist?

In any given area, between 85 and 95 percent of all the houses for sale. This is why the multilist is so important. Right from its pages, you can plot much of your house-hunting strategy.

"Without benefit of the multilist, we decided to try the drive-around approach. Since our target area was limited, we figured we could keep an eye on the market through the car windows. After one week, we gave up. It took too much time."—C.A.

Can I buy the multilist books?

Not unless you are an actively practicing real estate agent.

49

Where can I see the multilist?

At all participating real estate offices. Most agencies do participate.

How often does a new multilist come out?

Every week in most parts of the country, usually on the same day each week.

"Our agent's office was several miles from our home. We asked him if he could arrange with a closer branch for us to drop in weekly and check the multilist. He arranged it, and saved us a lot of travel."—J.H.

How current is the multilist?

It contains all houses except those listed within the past week. The week's lag is due to printing and publishing time.

What about the homes just coming on the market?

The multilist is supplemented by a computer listing sometimes called the "hot sheet." Within twenty-four to forty-eight hours after a house goes up for sale, it is on the hot sheet. All participating agencies have the hot sheets. A daily review of these sheets can give you a slight jump on other buyers.

Sample Multiple Listing

Date Put on Market — **ML #91822S**

Cost Factor — **Price $71,900**

Potential Remodeling — **DR Poss. in place den**

Flexibility in Finances — **Assumable**

Seller Motivation — **Reason Retirement Poss. Settle.**

Cost Factor — **Total 512.60**

Photo

Condition — **Excellent starter home!**

Location — **Water Public**

Access — **To show: Call Office Key Lock Box**

Address 916 Hilltop Road, Hillsboro, USA				Price $71,900	
ML #91822S	Area 3	Dev. University Acres		Munic. Hillsboro	
Lot Size 62 x 213			Gar. 2 Car	Broker Code	CB 3½
Style Ranch	Constr. Stucco/Fr.	Sq.Ft.		Finc. Conventional	
Age 1951	Frpl. No	Bsmt. Full			

Rooms	No.	Lev.	Floor	Drapes
LR	1	1	HW	
DR	Poss. in place den			
KIT	1	1	Vinyl	
FR	1	LL	Tile	
BR	2	1	HW	
Bath	1	1	Vinyl	
PR				
Lndry	1	LL	HW	
Den	1	1	HW	
Enclosed porch (20½ x 7)				

Strms. Yes Scrns. Yes
Range Gas D/W No Disp. No
Heat Gas FHA H/W Gas
Cent/Air Yes ☐ No ☒
Handicap Facilities Yes ☐ No ☒
Zoning Res.
Home Warranty Yes ☐ No ☒
Mtg. Co. Clear
Water Public Sewer Public Public Trans.
RE Taxes: Net xxxxxxx Twp. $175.80 School $336.80 Total 512.60 Assumable ☐ Yes ☐ No Mtg. Bal.
School Dist. Hillsboro Pmt. Int. %
Remarks & Objections Excellent starter home! Surrounded by lovely larger homes. Some cosmetics would greatly enhance the value of this home. Nice deep lot with mature trees. Refrigerator and washer stay.
Directions: left on 9th St. right on Hilltop to house
To show: Call Office Key Lock Box Information though believed accurate is not guaranteed
Seller: John Doe Ph. 555-1111 Tenant Vacant Ph.
Broker Hillsboro Realty Ph. 555-5101 Agent John Hill Ph. 555-7150

This hypothetical listing shows the information on a multilist entry, in this case for a 1951 ranch house in Hillsboro.

Can I take a multilist book home?

Sometimes.

For real estate agents, the multilist is their bible. Some will let you take it home overnight. More likely, an agent will lend you last week's book. Even though a week old, it can be valuable to browse through. Most of the homes listed in it will still be for sale.

Is there a national multilist service?

No. However, multilist services are moving toward regionalization. For example, the Minneapolis and St. Paul services have merged. Buyers in the Twin Cities area can preview all listings in one book.

Does an agent from my area have access to multilists in other cities?

Yes. Through his contacts in other cities, he can request copies of multilist entries. He does not, however, have those books in his office.

MISCELLANEOUS STRATEGIES

Can I use word-of-mouth to find a house?

Yes. In a tight market, it can be as important as ads or the multilist.

"The listings were out-of-date in Seattle. Word-of-mouth was so important. We spread the word to friends, co-workers, brokers, even strangers, that we were looking."—E.F.

SEARCH STRATEGIES

Are house-wanted ads effective?

No. Most are placed by agents trying to get listings. If you place such an ad, prepare for a deluge of calls from agents wanting to represent you.

Is there much opportunity for me to rent a house with the option to buy?

Not much. You have to be in the right place at the right time.

Check the Houses-for-Rent ads. A few may actually say "rent with the option to buy." For those that don't, ask the owner to consider such an arrangement.

"We did a lot of window shopping first. Then we rented a house in the country to try it out. We knew the owner was going to sell it shortly."—C.C.

Should I look above my price range, in hopes of bargaining the seller down?

Look outside your price range, yes. But do not visit those houses, not yet.

When searching the multilist or ads, scan the homes listed at up to 15 percent above your price range. Record the address, price, date, and multilist number of any that really appeal to you. Do *not* visit them now. If you fall in love with one and can't afford it, you suffer needless agony. However, keep an eye on these houses. The prices of a few may eventually drop into your range.

"I kept my eye on a house which at first was well above our price range. After seeing two or three price drops in the ads, I decided to make an offer near the top of my range. After a counteroffer, I finally bought the house."—J.W.

What if the house I want is sold or disappears from the market?

Call the listing agent to see what happened. If the house was sold, you have two choices:

- Make a backup offer in hopes the first offer falls through.
- Watch for the house to resurface on the multilist. It does happen.

"We had driven by the house earlier with our agent. We liked it, but the agent said it was sold. Later, we found it back in the multilist book. The original buyer hadn't been able to get a loan. Our offer was accepted, and we bought it."—P.M.

"I clipped an ad for a duplex I liked. A month later I checked the multilist, and it was gone. I called the listing agency, and learned that the seller was vacillating. He had taken the house off the market temporarily. The agent checked with the seller. He agreed to show us the house and entertain an offer. Though we did not make an offer, we were glad we checked it out. It gave us a good comparison property for future hunting."—C.A.

LONG-DISTANCE HUNTING

How do I find a house in another area?

The methods are the same as in local house hunting. Research your market, find a good agent, negotiate effectively, inspect carefully. However, the tactics are a little different.

How do I choose an agent for a long-distance move?

If you know a local agent, ask him to contact an agent in the city you are moving to.

Most real estate agencies have an agreement with a relocation company, a firm that finds agents in other cities. Your hometown agent will talk by phone with the new agent, and explain your needs. If he is satisfied that the new agent can help you, the new agent will be asked to call you within a day or two.

Even if you don't know an agent in your hometown, you can still drop into or call a local agency cold. Most likely the agency will be glad to put you in touch with an agent in another city.

Another tactic is to call the Board of Realtors in your new city. Ask them who the top one or two outfits are in their city. Also find out whether there are any buyer's agents in their area. Then call one of the agents or agencies, and explain your needs.

A third approach, if you have the time, is to visit the area first. Drive around and get acquainted with the housing types and neighborhoods. Once you have made some choices, locate an agency or two with listings similar to those choices. Then ask the manager to suggest an agent to help you.

What should I look for in a long-distance agent?

Ask for a Certified Residential Specialist (CRS). You will be getting a well-trained and experienced agent. If you have narrowed down the area somewhat, say, the southwest suburbs of Minneapolis, ask for a CRS familiar with that territory.

What should I ask the agent to do for me?

The same things you would ask a local agent.

Explain your wants and needs, and request copies of suitable multilist entries, a comparables file, and a street map of the area. Most agencies have kits prepared for out-of-towners, containing community profiles, tax and utility information, plus lists of health and recreation facilities. Be sure the kit contains the information you need.

How do I explore the market firsthand?

You have three choices:

- Buy now, after a quick search.
- Rent, and look around.
- Lease, and try out a place.

There are pros and cons to each.

Buy now. If you want to buy immediately, get a motel or hotel for a week. Then proceed to scout the market as you would in Search Preparation. You can line up an agent before you get to town, or find one

SEARCH STRATEGIES

after you arrive. To save time, most buyers prefer to have one lined up.

The buy-now approach saves you from paying rent. However, you are relying heavily on the agent in selecting a neighborhood. And your deadline puts you in a weak negotiating position.

Rent and search. Find a neighborhood or community that meets your needs. Rent a house or apartment while you look for a place to buy. Set a deadline to buy, say four to six months. This gives you time to know the area and the people. You don't lose a lot of rent, but you do have a double moving bill. Few rental agreements are month-by-month, so your opportunities for this approach are limited.

Lease with option to buy. A portion of your monthly rent goes toward the purchase price. If you like the house and community, you buy the place within two to five years. You are trying out not only the house but also the community. The disadvantages are that you lose some rent, and the opportunities to lease are limited.

"During our first trip to Minneapolis, we did not meet with any realtors or look at specific houses. We wanted to scout the various neighborhoods, housing types, and rental units. We were planning to buy, if not immediately, then very shortly after moving to Minnesota."—J.W.

3

Choosing an Agent

Shouldn't house hunting begin with finding an agent?

The answer is no, especially if you are buying a house for the first time. In any "hiring" situation, you should know a little about the field. Then you will know what to look for in the person to be hired. Picking a real estate agent is especially tricky. You are looking for a combination best friend and real estate professional.

You will be explaining your needs to him, revealing your financial situation, traveling with him, and calling him at all hours. You will be looking for a combination market researcher, negotiator, legal eagle, financial adviser, and project coordinator.

CHOOSING AN AGENT

If you find this combination in a day or two, you have either the wisdom of Solomon or a good stroke of luck.

However, if you have followed the steps in Search Preparation and Search Strategies, you may have some good leads by now. In this chapter you will gain tips on narrowing your choice.

AGENTS AND AGENCIES

What is a real estate agent?

A person licensed by the state to sell houses and other real estate. He is an "associate" of the agency, a self-employed person who may use the facilities and advertising of the agency. In turn, he gives part of his sales commissions to the agency. The agent works for the person who pays his commission: the seller.

What is a listing agent?

An agent who enters into an agreement with a homeowner to help sell his house. He does this by advertising and showing people through.

How does a listing agent get his assignment?

Mostly from "farming" a certain area, perhaps the community where he lives. Agents farm an area by contacting homeowners to see if they are planning to sell. Secondary sources of assignments include handling phone inquiries to his agency, and referrals from former clients.

How do I choose a real estate agency?

Look for one in the classifieds with several listings in your price range and neighborhoods that interest you.

There is much overlap among agencies in this regard. To sort them out, inquire about their training programs and years of operation. Also, get referrals from friends who have dealt with the agencies. Finally, bankers, lawyers, and appraisers might give you some additional leads. They often hesitate to name individual agents, but may suggest an agency.

Can a national franchise help me better than a local outfit?

There is little difference.

A national franchise, such as Century 21, consists of local offices. In long-distance house hunting, the national franchise contacts its counterparts in other cities. But a local, nonfranchise agency can do the same thing with a sister relocation agency.

Do certain agencies have specialties?

Not usually. The real estate market is so competitive that few agencies can afford to specialize. They must go after every home that might hit the market.

If their agents live in certain communities and farm them, an agency may have more listings than usual in those communities. A few agencies specialize to a

CHOOSING AN AGENT

degree in expensive housing. They get sales in that market, and through referrals build up a reputation among the wealthy.

Do some *agents* have specialties?

A few do specialize. Some agents like the challenge of dealing with long-distance movers. If you are one, you might ask an agency manager if there is such a specialist in his office.

Another infrequent specialty is first-time home buyers. An agent gets one or two. Then through referrals, all of a sudden he has several first-timers.

What happens when I call a real estate office?

You will get the duty agent. He is a real estate agent who answers the agency's incoming calls during his two- to eight-hour shift of phone duty.

Will the duty agent become my agent?

Only if you want him to. Phone duty is not assigned according to agent quality. You may get a good one or a bad one. It's a roulette game.

If you have a very specific idea of what you want in a house and location, ask for the manager. Tell him your needs, and request that he match you with an agent who knows the most about your market. The more specific you can be, the less likely he is to assign you to one of his buddies, or to an idle agent.

LOCATING A GOOD AGENT

How do I locate a good agent?

There are three ways to get leads on agents:

- Locating a good agency, and then finding the right agent for you.
- Getting referrals from satisfied customers and others in the field.
- Learning of an agent accidentally, while out house hunting.

None of these is guaranteed to produce the perfect agent for you. Perhaps more important is what you find out about the agent after you've been given a lead, because you want a *good* agent, one who works well with you.

About half of buyers find agents through friends or relatives who have recently bought houses. Others may find the right agent only after getting out on the house-hunting trail. Open houses and referrals from bankers and others in the real estate field tend to be the least effective sources.

Whichever method you choose, be aware of the following pitfalls:

- Asking friends for referrals. Remember that an agent who works well with one person may not work well with you. Find out *why* the agent is being recommended.
- Open houses. A very slow way to look for agents, and it doesn't resemble the real house-hunting situation.

- Listing agents. Scrutinize their behavior. If you like one, ask questions about his background. But don't automatically commit yourself to him, despite pressure to do so.

- Recommendations from professionals in related fields. Surely bankers, insurance agents, and others must have some great suggestions. But most will hesitate to give you a referral. Some feel it would pose a conflict of interest with their work.

When I get a lead, how should I contact the agent?

Phone his office. If he is not in, leave a message for him to call you. (This presumes that you have never met him.)

What is the first thing I should mention in our conversation?

Indicate your housing needs and your timetable. If you need a house in a hurry, be sure to specify your deadline to the agent. Ask him if he can meet that deadline. If he can't, because of his workload, he will refer you to another agent. But the supply of agents usually exceeds the demand of buyers, especially from October to March. Even during the peak sales months of May to August, few agents become overloaded.

Even if you aren't in a hurry, you'll still want assurance that an agent is available when you need one. Set up a few ground rules about absences. For example, stipulate that your agent will turn you over to another temporarily in the event of vacation, death in the family, out-of-town seminars, and so on.

What warning signals should I be alert to when I first talk to an agent?

The signals won't be obvious. But have your antennae out for any of the following:

- The agent doesn't ask in detail about your needs. Seems ready to start showing you houses at once.
- He gushes enthusiasm until he hears how much you can afford, then he cools off.
- He's impatient. You'll need someone you can get along with.

SCREENING AN AGENT

Should the agent's personality be a factor in my selection?

Very much so!

You may be practically "going steady" with your agent for several weeks. You want to feel comfortable asking questions and making requests. It takes some buyers several months to find an agent they connect with. Others find compatible agents right away.

Also, picture how the agent might get along with you and a seller during the critical negotiation and closing phases. One buyer credited her agent's warm personality in helping her and the sellers reach agreement on touchy issues of major repairs and a postponed closing date.

"We asked her over to our house, to explain our needs and learn her background. Then we drove her around, and showed her some houses we liked. Could she help us find something similar? She felt she could, and so we agreed to take her on."—E.F.

What should I look for in the way of training?

All agents have to pass a written examination administered by your state insurance commission. The exam emphasizes home financing, probably the trickiest part of an agent's job. Once he passes the state exam, the agent can become associated with a real estate agency.

Does the agency provide any training?

You will have to ask.

Some agencies offer intensive training programs, lasting a month or more. During that time, the new agent cannot take on clients. Other agencies do not offer such programs, and throw the greenhorn into the market cold.

Is continuing education a clue to picking an agent?

Yes, it's very important.

As a minimum, look for a graduate of the National

Association of Realtors' Realtor Institute. Designated a GRI, the realtor has completed the institute's rigorous three-week course, plus a certain number of real estate transactions.

The next step up the ladder is the Certified Residential Specialist, or CRS. He has completed college courses in real estate and closed deals beyond those required of the GRI.

Finally, there are the broker and associate broker. They have passed a more comprehensive state exam.

Can an experienced agent serve me better?

Actually, since the greenhorn probably has fewer clients at this stage, he may be able to devote more time to you. If you plan to spend a lot of time looking or have a tight deadline, this will be important to you.

But the difference between the greenhorn and the old pro often comes down to experience in financing. Both should know how to finance deals where only a private lender is involved (i.e., no government-insured loans). However, on loans by private lenders involving government backing, the old pro will (or had better) know the procedures. The greenhorn may have to get help from his supervisor on the deals.

In other ways, the old pro and the greenhorn are about equally effective. Remember that the agent's job is to help you obtain critical financial information and deliver your offer. He does not do any negotiating.

Can a broker serve me better?

A qualified yes. However, most of the agents are salesmen rather than brokers. Many of the brokers are

CHOOSING AN AGENT

busy supervising offices. Therefore, your chances of getting a broker are not too good.

The broker must have a certain number of years' experience and must have made a certain number of transactions. He must also have college credits in real estate. The salesman needs little or no college credit. He may or may not be more experienced than the broker. Some salesmen have many years of experience and are very good.

Are the big sellers the better agents?

Sales volume has some connection with quality. However, it is far less important to you than personality and training.

One million dollars in annual sales used to be the mark of a highly successful salesman. Now, it is more like one and a half to two million. But many good agents sell less than this.

Can I ask an agent what his sales volume was for the past year?

You can, but be careful. This may be a sensitive subject. Therefore don't ask about sales volume at the beginning of your initial conversation. Later in the discussion say something like "How many transactions did you complete this past year? Would you mind telling me the dollar amount?"

How much should my agent know about financing?

A lot.

The best way to find out what he knows is to ask

some questions. Has he taken some advanced training in financing? Can he answer concerns about financing that have crossed your mind during the preparation stage: questions on mortgages, including your conditional mortgage, or questions on the financial aspects of your trial sales contract.

If you are a first-time home buyer or have a limited income, ask him about government loans. They exist, and he should know about them. Has he ever closed a deal that involved a government-insured loan? If you are looking into alternative financing, ask him for suggestions on methods that appeal to you, for instance, joint ownership and financing.

If you are unsure about choosing a fixed or adjustable-rate mortgage, ask his opinion. There are no pat answers to this question. If he gives you one, beware.

Many buyers have done relatively little homework on financing the sale. When it comes time to get a loan, they often take the agent's first suggestion. If you ask an agent's opinion, do some homework yourself, to see if his suggestions will work for you.

Can I try out more than one agent at the beginning of my search?

Yes. Use proper etiquette, however.

You may ask the manager of an agency to suggest two agents who might suit your needs. Then interview them. If you like them both, you can try them both out. Tell the agents what you are doing. Specify a date when the trial period will end. At that time one, or neither, of them is selected. A few agents may refuse such an arrangement. But most, needing the clients, will honor your request.

CHOOSING AN AGENT

You can also use this procedure to try out one agent from agency A, and another from agency B. Again, tell them what you are doing and when the trial period will end.

Can I use several agents throughout the search?

Though most house hunters eventually settle down with one agent, a few play the field, using several agents. If you opt for this route, as a courtesy be sure to tell each agent that you are working with others. This will make some agents work harder for you, but will turn others off.

4

Working with an Agent

In this chapter you will learn the procedures, etiquette, ethics, and pressures in the agent–client relationship. To develop a good working relationship, immediately establish procedures for working together.

Perhaps the hardest thing is asking for something. You aren't paying the agent directly for his services, unless it's a buyer's agent. Therefore, you may feel you are imposing. Don't, as long as you do not overstep the procedures that you and the agent have agreed upon. Remember, you help pay his commission when you hand over your down payment to the seller.

MEETING WITH THE AGENT

What should I do when meeting with my agent?

Your purpose in meeting is for him to know you better, and to set the house hunting in motion.

Your first meeting should cover the following:

- Wants and needs. Give him a copy. Describe your family's interests in detail.

- Finance. Show him your "qualifying" figures and your conditional mortgage approval.

- The market. Review multilist entries with him, pointing out houses of interest in your price range.

- Timing. Ask the agent how long it might take to find and buy the type of house you want. If you have a deadline, ask how realistic it is in light of the market. If you don't have a deadline, establish a rough target date. This gives you both a time frame in which to work.

- First inspections. Agree on a date. If you have a good sense of what you want, ask the agent to do a computer run on all houses that might meet your needs, for example, all three-bedroom, single-family houses in northern Hillsboro listed between $55,000 and $80,000. But leave room for suggestions by the agent.

- House selection. Decide how you will select houses to visit first. With the agent, reviewing the multilist? At home, reviewing computer runs and ads?

Do I pay my agent a fee?

No. His commission comes from the seller.

"Buyers must understand the agent's situation. It's no benefits and all commission. Give her your full support, and she'll work hard for you."—J.V., agent

Do I sign a contract with the agent?

No. But discuss what you expect of him, and list the items on paper. Make sure to establish some ground rules, especially on contacting each other and handling information requests. For instance:

- Contact. Establish a method (phone, personal call) and frequency for contacting each other.

- Reaction time. Agree on how fast the agent will react to your requests.

- Listings update. If you want a computer printout every day at 10 A.M., specify that. (You pick it up, of course.)

- Multilist copies. When inspecting a house, have the agent provide you with a copy of the multilist entry.

- Lawyer. Reserve the right to have a lawyer check over any contracts.

"Whenever we had requests, we would call our agent's home answering service. She would get back to us right away."—S.Z.

Can I change agents?

Yes. Tell your new agent *why* you dropped the old agent. Describe what house hunting you've already done.

Some buyers hesitate to tell a new agent they are switching for fear they will sound fickle. This fear is groundless. An agent will not hold the switch against you.

How soon should I be seeing houses after meeting the agent?

The very next day, if you are in a hurry.

Don't, however, expect to visit houses the same day. The agent must make arrangements for the visits.

PREPARING TO VISIT HOMES

Who picks the houses?

You should. However, your agent can help you narrow down the field in three ways:

- Help you locate entries in the multilist that meet your needs.
- Do a computer run of all homes for sale of a certain type.
- Contact listing agents with your questions.

How often can I ask my agent to consult his computer for new listings?

Every day, particularly if it's a tight market.

How does my agent see a house before showing it?

This depends on whether it's listed with his agency or not.

His agency listings. Each week, your agent inspects new listings of his agency. In some states, the host listing agent must provide a list of defects supplied by the seller. Ask your agent if he has such a list.

Other listings. The only way your agent gets to know houses outside his agency's listings is by reading the multilist, calling the listing agent, or visiting with a client. Ask your agent if he has ever been in the house.

"Our agent wasn't aggressive enough. She didn't preview some that she should have. One house she took us to was awful, in terrible condition."—W.D.

Will my agent try to steer me toward his agency's listings?

Probably not. For years home-buying books have warned about such practices. But buyers are not finding this to be a problem. The multilist makes it easy for you to select listings from any agency.

How do I get details on houses in the classifieds?

Ask your agent to call the listing agents or sellers. Tell him what you need to know. This will save you a lot of phone time in the long run.

"Most of our leads came from newspaper ads. We would call our agent. She would call the listing agent and find out what we wanted to know, for example, yard size, number of rooms, finished basement. It saved us a lot of calling."—S.Z.

How many houses should I inspect in a day?

Usually no more than four. Five on rare occasions, if you are in a hurry to buy.

If you see too many houses too quickly, they start running together in your mind. You forget which kitchen goes with which living room. Also, you need time between houses to talk over your impressions with your spouse, partner, or agent.

Does my agent make the appointments?

Yes, in two ways:

Lock box. If there is a lock box at the house, your agent can use his master key to open the box and get the house key. This way you can visit the house almost any time. The multilist tells whether a lock box exists.

No lock box. Your agent calls the listing agent or seller to make arrangements to get in.

Should we arrange to have the seller home when we visit?

Most agents prefer the seller *not* be home. However, buyers are divided on this issue. Here are the reasons pro and con.

Reasons against having seller present. You feel freer to snoop around, open closet doors, and turn on water faucets. If at home, some sellers may follow you around. Others may talk too much, perhaps prematurely killing a deal.

Reasons for having seller present. The seller can answer questions that your agent cannot. Who are the neighbors? Does the basement leak during a rainstorm? You can always have your agent phone these questions to the seller. But sometimes you lose something in the translation. Also, if the seller is home, you may pick up clues on how motivated he is to sell.

Should my agent inspect a property before I do?

In some areas, it is common for an agent to "pre-inspect" any home before showing it to his client. But this is not necessary unless the place is unique (for instance, it contains several outbuildings) or you are uncertain of the condition it's in. In these cases, ask your agent to tour the place with the seller the day before your appointment. Instruct him on what to ask. Then, with answers in hand, you can leisurely tour the place without the seller present if you like.

WORKING WITH AN AGENT

INSPECTING HOUSES WITH THE AGENT

What does the agent do?

Not much. The house should sell itself. He should talk and trail you around as little as possible. But he should be available to answer questions. The agent's most important moves were back in the office, lining up houses.

Should my agent look for defects as I inspect the house?

Yes. He is ethically bound to be more than a spectator. If he sees a water stain on the kitchen ceiling, for example, he must ask the seller about it and give you an answer. If you discover something questionable, point it out to your agent. Have him check on it.

Can my agent answer questions on major repairs and their costs?

Not unless he has a professional background in home construction and maintenance, which he probably does not.

If you ask about major repairs, your agent should direct your question to the seller or suggest that a professional look over the problem. Unfortunately, agents sometimes offer advice beyond their capabilities. Sensing that buyers want quick answers, they may offer "solutions" on such weighty matters as raising roofs, knocking out walls for picture windows, and expanding the heating system. Rely on experts, not your agent, to answer these questions.

77

Can I ask the seller questions?

Yes. If you want this option, make it clear to your agent before entering the house.

Some agents prefer that you channel your questions through them. But many don't mind if you ask the seller directly. If the seller is hanging around as you inspect the house, he may be receptive to questions.

What kinds of questions can I ask the seller?

Just about any pertaining to the house, neighborhood, or the seller's reason for moving. Of special interest to buyers are questions about home condition and the neighborhood.

Condition. If it's an older house, you will want to know about age and upkeep. How old is the place? How long has the seller lived there? Has the house been treated for termites? How old are the roof, plumbing, wiring, heating system, and water heater? Are any warranties still in effect? Are any appliances to be included in the sale?

Neighborhood. Are the neighbors quiet? Do they have children? Are there neighborhood get-togethers? Is there a barking dog next door? Usually, only the seller can answer these questions. Feel free to ask him.

Can I talk to the seller of an unoccupied house?

Yes. Ask your agent to arrange for you to phone the seller. If the previous owner died, ask your agent to locate relatives who have been in the house. However, if no one knows the house well enough to answer your questions, you may have to get a building inspector for an assessment.

If the agent knows a seller is lying, can he tell me?

Definitely. To do otherwise would violate his code of ethics.

Remember, if the seller gave the listing agent a list of defects, you can learn what's wrong *before* the inspection. After the visit, ask your agent if anything the seller said doesn't ring true.

Should my agent drive me from house to house?

Yes. And while he is driving, make an immediate evaluation of the last house visited.

If you are with a spouse or partner, let your agent listen in on your conversation. Don't speak in whispers. The more the agent knows about your reaction, the better he can direct you to homes you might like. In fact, a good agent should be asking you questions: what you think of the kitchen, the yard, the neighborhood, and so on.

Can I call the seller after the visit?

You can, but this gets into a question of agent–client etiquette.

If you visited the house with an agent, you should

direct your questions through the agent. This way, the seller is not at the beck and call of dozens of potential buyers.

Legally though, you can call the seller. Some buyers do, especially when faced with a tight deadline or competition for the house. You will have to decide whether expediency outweighs etiquette. Remember that proper etiquette will help you keep an amiable relationship with both your agent and the seller.

Can I go back to a house without my agent?

You can, but again it's a question of etiquette. If you are anxious to see the house again, and your agent is not available, ask his pinch hitter to go with you, as the representative of your agent, of course. If he balks, ask the manager to assign someone.

How soon can I go back to a house I like?

The same day, if it can be arranged.

How many times can I return to a house?

As many times as you want. But if you plan your visits well, two or three trips are the most you will need. If you find yourself going back five or six times, something is wrong with your inspections procedure.

How can I inspect a house most effectively on a return trip?

Make a checklist of things to inspect. Here's a sample checklist:

WORKING WITH AN AGENT

_____ How big is the back porch?

_____ How many windows are in the dining room?

_____ Where is the rear property line?

_____ Does the air conditioner work?

_____ How high are the ceilings?

_____ Is the west bedroom shaded in the afternoon?

What is my agent's role once I've begun negotiations?

Your agent can help you in the following ways:

- Advise you on what is customary procedure in your area.
- Help you locate experts as needed.
- Attend important meetings with you, such as the loan application meeting.
- Keep track of progress, and speed things up if necessary.
- Alert you to problem areas that need checking out, such as radon gas.
- Make deposits according to your specifications.
- Make deliveries and pick up requested information, such as inspection reports.

Your agent's job doesn't end once you have found a house you like. His roles will be covered in greater detail in later chapters.

The agent will earn several thousand dollars in commission when you buy a house. So use him as needed at each stage, right through the closing.

"A buyer should never feel a sense of obligation to buy a house, just because the agent has spent a lot of time with him. The agent also wants the right fit between buyer and house, so he can get more referrals."—M.L., agent

ETHICS AND THE AGENT

Is my agent bound by a code of ethics?

Yes. In each state, the licensing procedure includes a code of ethics. In addition, agents who are members of the National Association of Realtors are bound by that organization's code of ethics.

What unethical practices are listed in codes of ethics?

Your agent cannot do the following:

- Make false promises to you, or "substantially" misrepresent a property.

- Represent both you and the seller in a deal, without your written consent.

- Deposit your money in a manner violating code requirements, for example, in his name rather than in that of his supervising broker.

- Accept compensation for your deal from anyone except his supervising broker.

WORKING WITH AN AGENT

- Discriminate against you because of race, color, religious creed, sex, ancestry, national origin, or physical handicap.

Although some agents engage in pressure tactics, or "salesmanship," few cross the line into unethical behavior. To do so could mean loss of license.

What are the most common types of unethical, or borderline, practices?

Most of the unethical behavior comes from ignorance, often caused by inexperience. Not depositing your money in exactly the prescribed manner is an example.

Some unethical behavior stems from lack of communication with the buyer. For example, if you see a house with one agent, you cannot go back to that house with another agent. However, if the latter agent doesn't know you've been there, he won't know he is violating the code by accompanying you.

Might my agent try pressure tactics on me?

The best agents avoid such tactics and let the house sell itself. But even the best may drop a phrase or two to nudge you along toward a decision. Here are a few:

- "If I could, I'd buy this house myself."
- "Remember, other buyers are looking at it, too."
- "Interest rates are going up. Don't hold off too long."

- "We can make out an offer back at my office, and have it to the seller by 4 P.M." You haven't even said you want it.

- "How big shall we make the deposit?" You haven't even said you want to make one.

- "Yes, but don't you remember how big the basement is?" The "yes, but" deflects your attention from a problem you just brought up.

Don't be nudged into a decision before you are ready. Unless the market is tight, sleeping on a possible offer is a good idea.

"Our agent was also helping the seller look for a house. She was probably looking for a quick sale on both ends."—D.G.

"Our agent was pressuring us to get inspections and financing before the sale was firm. Every week she called up and said, 'Only one more week until the sale goes through.' She did this for two months. [This was a backup offer.]"—E.F.

"The agent pressured us into moving fast. She said that others had looked at the house, and gave us the impression that someone else would be making an offer in a day or two. She claimed that the sellers had come down $5,000 in their asking price. In hindsight, I'm suspicious of that claim, based on prices of similar homes in the area."—D.G.

WORKING WITH AN AGENT

Can I get mad at my agent?

You will have to gauge the personality of your agent.

For a very sensitive agent, one outburst may be enough to damage your relationship, regardless of whether you are in the right. Most agents, however, are thick-skinned enough to take one or two outbursts.

To avoid blowups, reach agreement in the beginning on what you expect of your agent.

When do I have a right to dismiss an agent?

Any time, for any reason. Even if you just don't like the agent's personality.

"I had worked with her about a year. When I dismissed her, I explained that I had psychologically gone through the wringer. I wanted to start afresh with a new agent."—E.F.

Can I switch to a better agent in the same office?

Yes. Do it through the agency manager, however.

Ask the manager to meet with your old agent and desired new agent, and explain that you want to switch. The manager will probably work out a split commission deal for the two agents, should your new agent help find you a house.

"I found an agent I liked, when he substituted one day for my regular agent. The substitute

85

was more easy-going, had grown up in the area I was hunting in, still lived there, and knew in advance which houses were going on the market. I wanted to switch to him. But I remained unhappily faithful to my old agent, not thinking that I could switch."—C.A.

5

Looking at Homes

Buyers like this part the best. It's the field trip, the payoff for earlier preparation. There are literally hundreds of things you could check out when looking at houses. This chapter is arranged so that you don't overlook the most important checks and conditions, the potentially fatal flaws.

When looking at used houses, you will find things aren't perfect. But always remember, your primary goal is to find the right kind of house in the right location.

BEFORE ARRIVING

What should I know about a house before entering?

The information on the multilist entry. Have a copy in hand when you enter. This saves the time of asking needless questions, and frees you to examine the place.

How long should I look over a house?

It depends on your personality. A stickler for details may need forty-five minutes or more; others may see enough in five to ten minutes. If you are a detail person, tell your agent this at the start. Then he can schedule and space your visits accordingly.

First, take a few minutes to go through the house and form an impression. If you feel at home, take whatever time you need to look at the details. But don't be overwhelmed by detail.

Remember! Your goal is to find the *kind* of house you want, *where* you want it.

"During a return trip to the stucco house, the agent told our daughter, 'Your parents take too long looking at a house.' She mentioned the remark when we got home. We were never very comfortable around that agent again. We should have told him right at the beginning that we like to take our time inspecting."—J.H.

"The buyer, and his agent, will know almost immediately if it is the house for him.

LOOKING AT HOMES

The agent should not point out features of the house. The house should sell itself."—M.L., agent

TOP INSPECTION PRIORITIES

Under what conditions should I walk away from a house I love?

There aren't many. But occasionally you'll find a problem where the cost of fixing up is prohibitive, or your potential loss too great. Leave a house you love if you encounter the following conditions:

- *Structurally unsound.* You rarely encounter this, but if you do, walk away. The cause may be faulty workmanship, poor soil conditions, or both. Look for these signs:
  —Foundation not square because of uneven settling. Major cracks and extensive crumbling result. This can distort the entire frame of the house, including walls, ceilings, and floors. All should be plumb, square and level. (Hairline cracks in foundation are not usually a problem.)
  —Too much sag in floors. Test by jumping on them. Sag indicates weak, rotten, or insect-infested supporting beams. Repairs are prohibitively costly.
  —Excessive sag or rot in attic rafters. Indicates serious structural defects below.

- *Overpriced home* for the neighborhood, like an $80,000 home in a $50,000 neighborhood.

You will have difficulty selling the house at what you paid for it. Neighborhood values tend to pull the top and bottom prices toward the norm. This condition is more common than the structurally unsound house.

- *Bad or insufficient drinking water.* Walk away from bad water, unless it can be improved with an ultraviolet treatment system.

  Even if the water is good, you'll need adequate flow (six gallons a minute minimum). You will use about seventy-five gallons a day per occupant. Ask local well-digging companies, city engineers, or neighbors whether shortages occur in dry months.

"I talked some friends into buying a fixer-upper. Then I watched them camp out for years in it, while slowly fixing it up."—J.S.

"We watched 'This Old House' on public television to learn how to inspect homes."—P.C.

In a *new* house, what is the most important thing to check?

Make sure everything is connected properly. Focus on the following, in this order:

- *Envelope* of the house: outer walls, roof, foundation. Is the siding straight and warp-free? Are windows caulked; do doors fit tightly? Is there insulation where you expect it? Are there water leaks?

- *Interior finishing.* Again, are things properly connected? Are moldings on straight? Do floor coverings meet in a straight line? Does any drywall patching show through?

- *Exterior grading* and seeding. Does the lot slope away for adequate drainage? Are downspouts properly situated? Is there adequate topsoil to support growth?

Mechanical systems in your new home are important, but are covered by warranties. Check them out, but focus on the above.

What's most important to examine in a *used* house?

The mechanical aspects become more important, but the envelope of the house is still the most critical item. Look at the following, in this order:

- *Envelope* of the house. Look for signs of instability. Are there major cracks in the foundation or outer walls? Are the corners vertical or plumb to the ground? Is the roofing worn, even coming apart? Are exterior walls smooth, firm, and weathertight? Are wood parts at least six inches off the ground to avoid termites and dry rot?

- *Electrical system.* Is there enough current for your needs? Minimum necessary current is 100 amps (check the fuse box). If you have an electric stove or oven, dryer, and central air conditioning, you need 150 to 200 amps.

Does wiring conform to code? Are all areas properly lighted, including steps and porches? Is the fuse box in good shape? Are there outlets on each wall? (rule of thumb: one outlet for each twelve feet of wall.)

- *Plumbing.* Is the water pressure adequate? Flush toilet while running water in two faucets. Are drains clogged or pipes leaky and rusty? Are there stains on the sink or ceilings below bathrooms, indicating hidden leaks?

- *Heating.* Is the system efficient? Ask seller for his winter heating bill. Then ask the supplier what the bill for a house that size should run. Are there blackened areas around the furnace, indicating unsafe operation? Do pipes leak or have rust? Does the furnace start to heat up the farthest room away within ten to fifteen minutes?

"Both the agent and seller claimed that the annual heating cost was about $500. But we never saw the bills. After we bought the house, the heating bills turned out to be nearly twice as much."—D.G.

CHECKING THE REST

How should I inspect the remainder of the house?

One building inspector begins at the top of the house and works down. Bad conditions above alert

LOOKING AT HOMES

him to possible causes below. Begin with the floor plan, then proceed from the top to the bottom of the house checking for the following:

- *Floor plan.* Are the four zones of the house (sleeping, living, eating, working) distinctly separated? Does traffic move from one zone to another without interfering with activities? Is the house situated so the living areas are bright and sunny?

- *Roof.* Are there loose and worn shingles? Look for places where the granular mineral coating is wearing away. Check in daylight, not at night with a flashlight. Is there flashing (shiny metal barriers) around the chimney or vent pipe and where two roof angles meet, to prevent water from entering? Are the gutters, downspouts, and extensions in good condition? (general rule: one downspout every thirty feet.)

- *Attic.* Are there water stains on the underside of the roof? Is there adequate ventilation to reduce moisture buildup in winter and heat buildup in summer? Is the attic damp and musty? Is the floor insulated? Are there bat, mice, or squirrel droppings? Is the attic reached by a stairway, or by a ladder through a trapdoor?

- *Interior walls, ceilings, and floors.* Are there bulges and large cracks in the walls and ceilings? Cracks indicate poor workmanship or uneven settling. (Hairline cracks are okay.) Are there stains indicating water seepage? Is the floor level? See where a marble rolls on wood or linoleum. Do the moldings separate from the floor (indicating shoddy construction or uneven settling)? What is the floor surface like? Look under linoleum and carpeting, if possible, for defects.

- *Windows and doors.* Do windows and screen doors provide adequate cross-ventilation and light? Are there storms and screens for all openings? Do they work? Do windows and

Home Inspection Worksheet

Date:
Address: Year built:

Structure	**Good**	**Needs Repair**	**Repair Cost**	**Comment**
Foundation				
Roof				
Siding				
Walls/Ceilings				
Floors				
Insulation				
Utilities				
Heating				
Water Heater				
Air-conditioning				
Plumbing				
Electricity				
Water Supply				
Sewage				

LOOKING AT HOMES

doors stick? Sticking indicates poor construction or uneven settling.

- *Basement.* Are there pools of water or water stains? This may be just downspout overflow, but could indicate a more serious seepage problem. Newly painted floors or cracks in foundation walls could also indicate water leaks. Is there a sump pump? If so, ask how often it is activated. Is there a damp and musty smell? It can often be corrected with a

	Good	Needs Repair	Repair Cost	Comment
Appliances				
Refrigerator				
Stove/Ovens				
Dishwasher				
Disposal				
Washer/Dryer				
Other				
Openings/Misc. Inside				
Windows				
Doors				
Shower/Tub				
Carpet				
Drapes				
Outside				
Landscaping				
Paved areas				
Drainage				
Garage				
Other				

Total Repairs: _____

dehumidifier. Are there large cracks in walls? Cracks could spell uneven settling. Do the cellar stairs have at least one handrail all the way down?

As you walk downstairs, look at the basement ceiling at eye level. This is your best vantage point for checking the levelness of the first floor.

- *Hot water heater.* Is there adequate capacity (forty gallons or more)? Are there puddles of water under it, indicating faulty operation? Does it heat properly? Check each hot water faucet.

- *Septic tank.* Has it been maintained properly? Ask for a record of tank maintenance. Does sewage surface in wet seasons? How big is the tank? It should have a capacity of at least 125 gallons a person.

"When you walk into a house, you'll know immediately if it's for you. You will fall in love on an emotional basis. After that, you and the experts can check out the functional stuff."—E.F.

Under what conditions can I sue for fraud after buying a house?

Several elements are necessary in a case of fraud. They include:

- Seller knowingly concealing a defect in the house. (If the seller doesn't know of the defect, there's no fraud.)

Life Expectancies of Housing Components

The following life expectancies are averages. Actual life will vary with care and climate.

Envelope of House

Foundation, frames of interior and exterior walls	life
Exterior siding: aluminum, wood, brick, stucco, stone, brick veneer	life
Roof: Asphalt shingles	15–25 years
Tile	30–50 years
Slate or metal	life

Interior Walls

Ceramic tile	life
Plaster	life
Dry wall	40–50 years
Wood paneling	40–50 years

Wood Floors (oak or pine) — life

Windows (steel or wood casement) — 40–50 years

Doors — 30–50 years

Wiring (copper, aluminum, Romex [nonmetallic]) — life

Pipes, plumbing

Copper	life
Galvanized iron	30–50 years
Plastic	30–40 years

Heating

Warm air furnace	25–30 years
Hot water boiler	30–50 years
Heating-duct work	40–70 years

Well and septic systems — 15–30 years

Appliances and Furnishings

Cabinets and vanities	18–30 years
Refrigerator	15–25 years
Commode	15–25 years
Electric range and oven	12–20 years
Water heater	10–12 years
Dishwasher	5–15 years
Washer and dryer	8–12 years
Carpeting	5–8 years

Costs of Major Repairs and Replacements

To avoid unnecessary costs, first find out what warranties exist on appliances and recent repair work. Have them signed over to you at the closing. Then check the figures below to see how much fixing up the place will cost.

Remodeling and Furnishings
Remodel kitchen	$5,000–$8,000
Remodel bath	$3,000–$6,000
Add single garage	$5,000–$8,000
Mason fireplace	$2,000–$4,000
Replace front door	$250–$600
Install storm door	$100–$200
Replace stove and oven	$400–$1,000
Replace refrigerator	$400–$900
Replace dishwasher	$400–$700
Paint interior walls and ceilings	$1,000–$5,000 (depending on size)

Exterior Work
Install new cedar shake roof	$2,500–$7,500
Install new asphalt shingle roof	$1,750–$3,500
Paint exterior of house	$500–$3,000
Install aluminum siding	$2,500–$6,000
Repoint brick exterior	$400–$1,000

Utilities
Increase electric service to 200 amps	$600–$1,500
Install new warm air furnace	$1,200–$2,500
Install new hot-water boiler for furnace	$1,500–$3,000
Install central air-conditioning compressor	$1,000–$2,000
Install hot water heater, 40 gal.	$400–$600
Dig new well	$2,500–$5,000
Dig new septic system	$2,500–$7,000

LOOKING AT HOMES

- Seller intent to mislead you, with you relying on the information.
- A resulting injury to you.

If it is all there and you can prove it, you've got a case.

However, if a defect can be seen by your naked eye and you fail to pick it up, you cannot claim concealment. That alone can cost you a fraud case. To avoid all this, make a careful inspection before the sale.

"Less than a month after we moved in, it rained hard and the roof leaked badly. I tried to locate the seller to get reimbursed to fix the roof. I called the agent and her supervisor for the seller's address and phone number. They said they didn't have it, and that there was nothing I could do. There was nothing in the contract to cover this problem. Still, I should have gotten the seller's address before he moved, in order to try for some compensation."—D.G.

6

The Offer

After you've found the house you want, the first step is to negotiate an offer. This is one of the three areas of house hunting that concern buyers most. Reactions at this time range from cold calculation to sheer panic.

The best way to overcome this fear is to know what to expect. This chapter addresses many situations that arise in making an offer, including some nontraditional ones. It shows you what steps to take in each situation.

All sorts of questions spin around in your head at this point. You may wish you had an army of experts by your side—lawyers, buyer's agents, inspectors, appraisers, street-smart friends.

THE OFFER

But wait! By this time you should be enough of an expert to handle this stage with only modest outside help. Yes, there are situations where you may need a lawyer or an appraiser now. But read on before putting out the call. When you know the steps, you can take them one at a time.

PREPARING TO MAKE THE OFFER

What should I know before I make an offer?

You have already collected most of the information you need. Let's summarize what you know:

- How much you can afford.
- How much similar houses are selling for.
- How motivated the seller is to sell, and perhaps how he set his price.
- What is right and wrong with the house.
- How the house suits your needs and wants.

Now you need to get some specific figures.

What figures do I need?

Ask your agent to return to his file of comparables. Have him find three to five recently sold houses that are most like the one you will make an offer on. If it's permissible, ask your agent to make you copies of the old multilist listings of these houses, so that you can study them in detail. Second, if you haven't already done so, ask the seller for copies of his utility bills and receipts for recent replacements and additions.

Now you should have nearly as much information as a professional appraiser, even though you don't have his trained eye or experience.

Let's say that the list of comparables ranged from $70,000 to $80,000 in purchase price. The list price on the house is $85,000. And you have discovered a potential $4,000 in needed repairs.

Now you should be able to come up with three figures:

- Your market value estimate $75,000
- Your bottom price (e.g., if the seller is highly motivated, you may be able to "steal" it for up to 25 percent off list price) $64,000
- Your top offer (based on your budget and your wants and needs) $77,000

Don't reveal these figures to your agent!

Shouldn't I get a professional appraisal before making an offer?

Only as a last resort. Instead, make your offer subject to a satisfactory building inspection. If you have plenty of time, no buyer competition, and a house with so many problems or unique features that it just isn't comparable, go ahead and get an appraiser—or a building inspector. But remember, it will cost you, and there is no guarantee that the seller will eventually accept your offer. If you do get an appraiser at this stage, try to hire one used by the lending institution that may be financing the deal.

"We looked at several houses, to get an idea of fair price, before even making an offer. That was about as good as getting an appraisal."—E.F.

How can I find out if anyone else is making an offer?

Ask your agent. He can tell you, or find out, if there are any offers pending. He may also be able to tell you the deadlines attached. He will not, however, be able to tell you how much the offers are. That would constitute a breach of contract between the seller and listing agent.

"In a tight housing market, the key is being mentally ready to move quickly. You may have to bid on a house the same day you see it. Try to find an agent who knows which houses are on sale before they are even listed."—F.M.

Can my agent help me with the amount I should offer?

No. He cannot suggest a dollar figure to you. That would be a breach of faith with the seller. However, you can ask the agent whether your offer is "in the ballpark" or utterly ridiculous.

If he does slip and suggest a figure, take it with a grain of salt. It may be on target, or it may be too high.

Can my offer be lower than the asking price?

Sure. This is not like shopping at Sears, where you are stuck with the list price. In most home sales, the purchase price is lower than the asking price—about 5 percent lower on average.

Does the price of the house make a difference in how low I bid?

Expensive homes tend to sell for less than list price, sometimes as much as 40 to 50 percent below list. On the other hand, low-priced homes, with more potential buyers, usually sell close to or even above the original asking price.

How low should I go?

Some books tell you to automatically knock off 10, 15, or even 25 percent of the list price in your first offer. A more realistic approach is to make a first offer 10 percent below your estimate of the market value of the house.

But this is no hard and fast figure. If the seller is anxious to get out, you might go considerably lower. Some investors make a living off property they buy at 25 percent or more below list price.

If you decide to try for a low figure first, perhaps your bottom price, don't let your agent know you are willing to go higher. His commission comes from the seller. If the seller asked your agent whether you would go higher, he would be obligated to say yes. Then the seller would likely reject your first offer.

THE OFFER

Will a very low offer make a seller mad—and end any negotiations?

Not necessarily. It depends on three things: why the seller is selling, how your agent presents the offer, and the price of the house. A very low offer is a calculated risk. But if the seller is highly motivated to sell, or if the agent tactfully presents your offer, negotiations should remain open.

If your agent gets sloppy and tells the seller, "I hate to present you with such a ridiculously low offer, but I must," then your chances of keeping the bargaining open are dealt a blow. Avoid this blunder by hiring a good agent in the first place.

Can I tell the agent how to present my offer?

Yes. Sort out with him those things that might make the seller more receptive. Are you a first-time home buyer, just beginning your family? That might strike a sentimental chord. Did you do your homework on the market and the condition of the house? Instruct your agent to tell the seller how you arrived at your offer. Submit those calculations in writing.

"I didn't know exactly what my agent was doing in presenting our contract. That bothered me."—P.C.

Can I ask my agent or the listing agent to take a cut in commission, in order to make an even lower offer?

Yes. Some agents will always refuse, but some may not. The agent may have to get approval from his supervising broker. The best time to try this tactic is when your offer and the seller's price are close together—and a reduction in commission might seal the deal. If you use this approach, apply the Golden Rule. Would you want someone to ask *you* to take a cut in pay in order to get a job done? Evaluate the situation in this light before employing the tactic.

Can I avoid *my* agent's cut of the commission by dealing directly with the seller?

Yes. If you find and inspect a house on your own, your agent is not entitled to a commission. That is, unless you then ask him to help you with the remaining stages of the purchase.

Can I avoid the *listing* agent's commission by dealing directly with the seller?

No. Even if the listing agent played absolutely no part in your purchase, he must get a commission from the seller. Otherwise, there would be a breach of contract between agent and seller.

THE OFFER

Should my offer ever be higher than the asking price?

Yes, that could happen. Here are three occasions in which you might consider topping the asking price:

- You know others are bidding on the house.
- You know from market conditions that it is underpriced and you want to make sure you beat the competition.
- You want certain concessions from the seller, such as major repairs or financing on the sale.

But in any event, don't go above your top offer price.

MAKING THE OFFER

How do I make an offer on a house?

Several ways:

- On a sales agreement, either preprinted or custom-made. It may be a short binder, or a full-length sales contract.
- An informal written offer, on a legal pad or even a scrap of paper.
- An oral offer, in person or on the phone.

There is really no one correct way. Buyers with tight deadlines who are dealing with sellers long-distance may make offers over the phone, then get the offers confirmed in writing. Someone buying directly from the seller may put the offer on plain white paper; when agreement is reached on price, a full-length contract is drawn up.

If you are dealing with an agent, you will usually be presented with a fill-in-the-blanks form, long or short, on which to make your offer. This is fine. Just be sure you understand all the wording.

What goes into my offer?

As a minimum, the price you are offering, a description of the property (address at least), a deadline for replying, and your signature. Either now or later, you will need to get *all* conditions of sale in writing.

Can the agent help me with the conditions attached to the offer?

Yes. He can advise you on what inspections, deposits, deadlines, and so forth to include. Though he cannot tell you who should pay for what inspections and for closing costs, he can tell you what is customary in your area.

Buyers rely heavily on their agents in this regard, perhaps too much. Each situation is unique, and *you* should ultimately make the decisions on what conditions will be in the contract.

Can I write an offer without my agent's or lawyer's help?

Yes. And if you are in a tight market and in a hurry, you may be tempted to. You can draw up a minimum offer (price, description of property, deadline) on your own. Those negotiating on a for-sale-by-owner house sometimes do. But when it comes to the full-length contract, with all conditions of sale, be sure to have an agent or lawyer help you.

Do I make a deposit with my offer?

A deposit indicates the seriousness of your offer. Even if it's not required by law, local custom may suggest some sort of deposit, however small. But if *only* custom is involved, you are not required to make any deposit, no matter how much your agent may pressure you to do so.

What are the chances that my first offer will be accepted?

Perhaps fifty-fifty. Most sales are agreed to by the third offer.

How can I improve the odds?

First of all, act as if your offer will be accepted. Don't say what you will do next to anyone, not even the agent. Make your offer look attractive and firm:

- Present a financial statement along with it.
- Indicate that you have conditional mortgage approval.
- Attach a deposit check.
- Don't ask for any extras, such as curtains or air conditioner. At this stage it may sound grabby.

- Play the psychology of numbers to your advantage. Offer $35,000 rather than $34,900, or $80,000 rather than $79,000.

Why should I present a financial statement with my offer?

You want the seller to have confidence in you—in your financial status in particular. You are asking him to take his house off the market while you arrange financing. If the seller is confident that you can get the loan or meet the mortgage payments, he'll be more likely to accept your offer.

Should a lawyer review my offer before I submit it?

As a general rule, have a lawyer review any real estate contract (sales, mortgage) before signing.

However, a lawyer's review is not always practical. Some questions: Can you get a lawyer fast? Are there other bidders? Will the seller wait for you? Can you spare the expense ($40 to $150 per hour)? If you can answer yes to all these questions, then do hire a lawyer to review your offer—not just the price, but also the financial terms, conditions of sale, and wording you don't understand.

In some places, such as New York City and other large cities, it is common practice to have lawyers review contracts. In small cities and rural areas, it's rare. Overall, only a small percentage of the buyers with agents have a lawyer review their offers.

A word of caution: Your agent may not be too happy to have a lawyer involved. In his eyes, the agent may

THE OFFER

see his control of the dealings slipping away. Make it clear when you first meet with your agent that you may be consulting a lawyer.

When *should* a lawyer review my offer?

If you have any questions about the offer, even after your agent has explained its contents, have a lawyer check it over. Likewise, if you are making an offer on a for-sale-by-owner house, you should have a lawyer's review.

Can I present or accept an offer subject to a lawyer's review?

Yes. This is occasionally done. If you take this precaution, be sure to do two things:

- Write "subject to lawyer's review" on the offer, and

- Include a tight deadline for review, say, no more than five working days from acceptance. Be forewarned that some sellers will balk at this condition, since it delays proceedings.

DELIVERING THE OFFER

How is my offer relayed to the seller?

If written, it will be hand-delivered by your agent to the listing agent, and then to the seller. It's just a matter of hours, or even minutes if all goes well. If you

111

are making an oral offer, your agent will simply phone the listing agent or the seller with your offer.

What if the agent says my offer is too ridiculous to deliver?

He can't refuse. By law, he must deliver any offer you make, no matter what he thinks of it.

If time is short, can I deliver my written offer to the seller rather than through my agent?

Yes. But in all likelihood he will drop everything to deliver it. And if he cannot, he can designate a fellow agent to make the delivery. In either case, he can phone the seller or listing agent and say that an offer is on the way.

How can I negotiate most effectively?

Follow some commonsense rules of good negotiating offered by author Sloan Bashinsky in his book *Homebuyers: Lambs to the Slaughter?*:

- Know as much about the seller as possible by asking questions about his circumstances.
- Disclose as little as possible about yourself.
- Get the seller and his agent to invest as much time in you as possible.
- Set a top limit in your mind, and stick to it.
- Be willing to risk losing the house.

THE OFFER

Remember, your top priority is getting the seller to agree on a purchase price. Record each offer, and the outcome, in a negotiating notebook.

Can I use a stand-in negotiator?

Yes, but beware. Negotiating can be the scariest part of house hunting, especially if you've never done it before. You may be tempted to call for help. That help can come from anyone—a buyer's agent, a lawyer, even your brother.

But think. Do they know your needs and financial situation well enough? Do they know the market as well as you? At this point, you are the best person to negotiate the offer.

How is a reply made to my offer?

Depending on how you made your offer, the seller will give you an oral or written reply. If you are using an agent, the agent will notify you.

When can I expect a reply?

It depends on what you stipulated in your offer. Usually twenty-four hours, perhaps forty-eight hours at the most.

What types of replies are possible?

The seller may do one of the following:

- Accept your offer.

113

- Decline your offer.
- Decline the offer but make you a counteroffer.

If the offer is accepted, what do I do?

If it was an oral offer and reply, get it in writing now, signed by both you and the seller.

If it was a written offer with few details, the next step is to hammer out a full-blown sales contract.

And if a full-length sales contract was used in the offer, make sure all changes are initialed by both parties, and all conditions have been put in writing. No verbal agreements, please! Then you and the seller each gets a copy.

If the seller makes a counteroffer, what do I do?

You have three choices:

- Accept it totally, and sign it.
- Accept the offer, with certain terms attached (such as, seller pays closing costs).
- Make a counteroffer.

Occasionally a seller or his agent may merely tell you that your written offer is too low. He will suggest that if it is raised a certain amount, it will be accepted. Do *not* raise your offer to verbal signals. Remind the seller that you have a formal offer on the table, and would appreciate a written counteroffer.

THE OFFER

"I made an offer at the top of my price range. The seller rejected it. A few days later, the seller's agent suggested that I make another bid. Just to play devil's advocate, I submitted another offer, a mere $100 above my original one. To my surprise, the seller accepted it."—J.W.

How do I make a counteroffer?

When you counter, write on a new form. Don't work with scratched-out figures or wording from the old form. Messiness can lead to confusion. However, save the old form in case a dispute arises. Keep in mind these tips when you counter:

- Remember what is not negotiable, and stick to it.

- Try to get something if you give up something (carpeting and drapes in exchange for upping your price).

- Raise your offer in small increments, just enough so that the seller feels progress is being made. In fact, you might make your increments smaller and smaller each time you raise, $80,000 to $82,000 to $83,000 to $83,500. This way it looks as if you're approaching your final "take it or leave it" offer, without your actually saying so.

- Don't announce a "final offer" unless you really are ready to drop the whole deal.

"In his counteroffer, the seller offered to do $1,000 in repairs. Our building inspector advised against accepting this condition, since the seller had screwed up several renovations."—E.F.

"After the inspection turned up several problems, we showed the seller a copy of the report. We told him we needed three to five days to reconsider the offer. The seller threatened to put the house back on the market, but did not. We made a counteroffer below our original price."—E.F.

In all of the above, keep in mind that your goal is to buy the house—not to win at the bargaining table. If you bargain too hard, you may lose the house.

If the seller says no and makes no counteroffer, is the deal dead?

Not necessarily. You may still submit another offer. But first ask your agent why the seller refused.

Can I talk with the seller during negotiations or after an offer is rejected?

Yes. You have the right to call the seller or deal with him face-to-face. If you want to meet with him, your agent may offer to arrange it and suggest that he be included. This is perfectly acceptable.

Sample Counteroffer

The sample counteroffer form below can be used by either the buyer or the seller. It is best suited for counteroffers in which only limited changes are requested. If you are making wholesale changes, retype the contract.

Counteroffer
Date: _____
In response to Offer to Purchase property known as _____
_____ made by _____ on [date], the following Counteroffer is submitted: _____
_____
_____

All other terms remain the same. This Counteroffer expires unless a copy with Seller's [Buyer's] written acceptance is delivered to Buyer [Seller] or agent on or before [time] on [date].
Signed: _____

Acceptance
Date: _____
The undersigned Seller [Buyer] accepts the above Counteroffer.
Signed: _____

Receipt of acceptance acknowledged on [date] by Buyer [Seller].

If the seller rejected my offer, can I persuade him to reconsider?

If you have done your homework, you should have some ammunition:

- The comparables and market value. Be ready with addresses, descriptions, and prices if you didn't present them with your first offer in detail. Your point: "I know the market, and this is what a house like yours sells for."

- Condition of the house. Present a list of items needing repair or replacement now or in the near future. Your point: "I'll have to put out some money soon to fix these problems. So I reduced my offer accordingly."

Are there negotiating no-nos?

When you're caught up in the emotion of negotiating, you might blurt out something that will backfire:

- "We can't afford any more." This might get the seller to worrying about whether you can finance the deal. Reserve this argument for your very last offer, if at all.

- "If you don't accept our offer, we'll buy the house over on Main Street." The seller's likely response: "Go ahead!"

- "I can't stand the wallpaper. We'll have redecorating expenses." Any personal insult is a good negotiation killer.

How early in the bidding game should I talk to the seller?

If you are confused about the seller's rejection or counteroffer, you may want to talk with him immediately. Or if you sense that your agent is causing things to bog down, you may want to take matters into your own hands. Most buyers do not find this drastic action necessary.

Wait a round or two until the seller has invested some time in you and knows you are serious. Then he will want to wrap up the deal.

THE OFFER

How can I keep my emotions in check?

Try these suggestions:

- Stick to the point when talking to the seller or agent. If you are trying to agree on the closing date, don't start arguing about shabby roofing.

- Refer often to your negotiating notebook, to stick to the facts. Use it to jot down your emotional reactions.

- Write down your points or proposals, and hand them to the seller. Don't shout them at him. Write down *his* proposals and study them. Don't automatically shake your head no.

Can other buyers make an offer while mine is being considered?

Yes. The seller could entertain dozens of offers at once, though it's very unlikely. If you stipulate a fairly tight deadline for replying—twenty-four hours is good—he will have less chance to receive competing offers.

If you are hunting in a really tight market, and need decisions fast, make sure you know where your spouse or partner can be reached. One couple lost out on a house because the wife was unable to reach her husband to talk over an offer.

What happens if the seller has two or more offers at once?

You may become engaged in a bidding war. There are two possible scenarios:

- *Successive bids.* One bid is already being reviewed, and another arrives. The listing agent will give the later bid to the seller to consider also.

- *Simultaneous bids.* Both bids arrive at the listing agent at the same time. This one is more complicated. The listing agent should (that is not to say that he will) return both bids to the bidders' agents, make each aware of the other bid, and ask if they want to change their bids before resubmitting. The agent cannot tell you the amount of the other bid.

Now, your move. Have your agent find out what the appraised value is if you don't already know. Keep in mind that if a bidding war yields an unrealistically high bid, the buyer may have trouble obtaining financing.

How does the seller respond in these situations?

In either case, the seller can do one of three things:

- Accept one of the bids.
- Make a counteroffer to one of the bids.
- Reject both bids, with no counteroffer.

THE OFFER

The listing agent will inform you of the seller's decision. If he rejects both offers with no counteroffer, you are free to submit another bid. But keep in mind the appraised and market values.

What proof do I have that there really is another bid?

Your agent may request to see a copy of the bid.

Are there ethical limits in a bidding war?

Yes. The seller must give all bidders an equal chance, by providing each with the same information. From the seller's point of view, a bidding war is good business. However, it could backfire if he pushes the bidders too far. He runs the risk that the bidders may simultaneously tire of the game and make no further offers. The seller is left empty-handed.

What tactics can I use to get my bid accepted?

Use the same ones you would in getting your first offer accepted. Only this time present your top offer, or within $1,000 of it. Make that offer on a full-length sales contract, if you did not before. Then the seller won't have to worry about what conditions and contingencies you might confront him with later.

Can I make an offer even if another buyer's offer is accepted?

Yes. But remember that once the seller has accepted that first offer, he cannot jump ship and snap up yours. You may have to wait two or three months to learn whether or not the first deal was consummated. One buyer did just that, and had her offer accepted when the first one fell through.

"We made a backup offer, and wrote out an earnest money check for $5,000. We wrote on the check 'not to be cashed until agreement is reached with seller.' The conditions of our offer included pulling out if we found another house, and obtaining satisfactory inspections on the house."—E.F.

7

Documents of Sale

After you've made your offer, your next concern is the documents regarding the sale of the house and your eventual possession of it. These documents fall into two main categories: the sales contract and the deed.

There are two ways to work out a sales contract. You can use a one-step procedure, in which the offer is presented along with all conditions of sale. Or you can use a two-step procedure, in which the offer is made on a short contract called a binder. After the offer is agreed to, you work out the details on a full-length contract.

Local custom usually dictates which procedure is followed. If one seller is used to one method, he may hesitate to negotiate using another.

The contract specifies what type of deed you will get. In this chapter you will learn what a deed is, which deeds are acceptable, and which to avoid.

THE BINDER AND EARNEST MONEY

What is a binder?

A binder is a short sales contract. It states only the essential terms of the offer and any deposit made.

With the binder, you and the seller agree to work out a complete sales contract within a specified time, usually five business days. If you use a binder, write in the precaution, "This agreement is subject to a contract within five business days."

Is a binder used in all home-buying deals?

No. In some parts of the country, it is not customary.

However, it can legally be used anywhere with an offer to purchase a house. It is often used when the details of the full sales contract are too complex to work out at the time of the offer. In a tight housing market the binder process is too slow, and the seller will favor a full sales contract.

Technically, your agent should deliver your offer any way you want to make it. However, in areas where the binder is rare or unknown, agents may refuse to break tradition and deliver a binder offer. Often this is for good reason. The agent knows what will and won't work with local sellers. Therefore, consider both tradition and buyer competition when deciding on the form of the offer.

DOCUMENTS OF SALE

What's in the binder?

At least four items:

- Purchase price (the offer).
- Description of the property.
- Amount of deposit.
- Signatures of buyer and seller.

The binder serves as your receipt for the earnest money.

Is there a standard form for the binder?

No. But it might look something like this:

Sample Binder

The Offer.
The Seller of house at _____ acknowledges receipt of $_____ as good-faith deposit from Buyer. The total price of house is $_____ . A formal agreement will be executed before [date].

Failure to Negotiate. If Buyer does not execute the agreement on or before the above date, Seller shall keep the deposit as damages. If Seller fails to execute an agreement on or before the above date, Seller shall return the deposit to Buyer.

Attachments. Any conditions to this offer shall be signed by both parties and attached.

Acceptance: [date].

Seller _____   Buyer _____

Seller _____   Buyer _____

What is earnest money?

A deposit attached to your offer, indicating your seriousness.

Is earnest money required with my offer?

No, aside from court-ordered sales.

No law requires you to make a deposit of a particular size, or any deposit at all. However, it might be expected in your locality.

How is the amount of earnest money determined?

By local custom.

In some areas, it is a token payment of about $50 to $200; in others, it's as much as 5 to 10 percent of your offer. The idea is to compensate the seller for taking his house off the market. The tighter the market, the more earnest money you should put up. If the market is very slow, a token payment may suffice.

If you don't have enough money on hand for a deposit, attach a promissory note, payable at the closing.

"We didn't have enough cash to hand over for a 5 percent deposit with our offer. I asked the seller if he would take a promissory note for about $1,750. He agreed to. At the closing, after all the papers were signed and money distributed, the seller ripped up the note."—P.M.

DOCUMENTS OF SALE

To whom do I make out the check?

To the supervising broker or agency of the seller's agent.

Where does my earnest money go?

Into an escrow account held by the broker.

With an escrow account, a third party (the broker) holds your money until the conditions of sale are met. So that your money is properly handled, write the following into your contract:

- The check shall be deposited only after the offer has been accepted.
- The money shall be returned within a certain number of days (say, five) if the deal falls through.

Do I get interest on my earnest money?

You can. Ask whether the broker routinely deposits earnest money in an interest-bearing account. If not, insert that requirement into your offer.

What if the seller fails to negotiate satisfactorily with me?

You can sue. You have to prove that the seller failed to respond promptly and completely to your offers and conditions. But if the seller returns your earnest money, suing is probably not worth the effort.

Can the seller deal with someone else after accepting my binder offer?

No, not during the time specified by the binder.

THE SALES CONTRACT

What is a sales contract?

It's a document specifying that you and the seller agree to the sale of the house and all conditions of the sale. This is your most important document.

Must the contract be a part of the offer?

No. It can be negotiated after the purchase price is agreed upon.

In your area it may be customary to include your offer in a full-length sales contract. But let's assume your offer has already been accepted.

Is there a standard contract?

No. Many contracts are on a fill-in-the-blanks, preprinted form, perhaps made up by your local Board of Realtors or a title insurance company. But yours could be on a scrap of paper or an index card.

Some preprinted sales contracts are written to protect the seller, not the buyer. They often lack even the most basic clauses for your protection. If you use one, review it carefully.

"We were renting with the option to buy. On a legal pad, we wrote a note agreeing to buy the

DOCUMENTS OF SALE

house for $40,000, with a portion of the rent going to the down payment. We also agreed on paper to find financing within three months. We and the sellers signed the note."—C.C.

"The sales contract was drawn up by our agent. I signed it. Then our agent sent it to the buyers to sign. The next day I received a telegram from the buyers simply stating, 'We agree to accept your offer.'"—C.F.

Who prepares the contract?

You and your agent or lawyer should do it. This way you are setting down the conditions first, rather than reacting to the seller's terms.

In some areas, it is customary for the seller and his lawyer or listing agent to draw up the contract. But it is not a legal requirement. Feel free to reverse the procedure.

What parts of the contract are not negotiable?

None. All parts are negotiable. Customarily, building and termite inspections and an appraisal will be required by somebody (a lender or municipality). These must be inserted into the contract.

What provisions should I make sure are in the contract?

Every contract *must* have the following:

- Date.

- Names of each buyer and seller.
- Price.
- Address of the property being sold.
- Date and place of the closing. (This is often changed later by mutual agreement.)
- Signatures of each buyer and seller.

Most contracts also have several or all of the following:

- Kind of deed that is to convey title.
- Mortgage contingency clause.
- Home inspection contingency.
- Pest (or termite) inspection contingency.
- Radon inspection contingency.
- Promise of clear title.
- Right of assignment (of contract to another buyer).
- Handling of deposits.
- Closing costs allocation.
- Personal property included in sale.
- Liability and maintenance of house (by seller) until closing.
- Adjustments on dividing taxes and utility bills.
- Appurtenance clause, stating that all plumb-

ing, heating, electrical, and built-in fixtures remain.

- Removal of debris provision.
- Day-of-closing inspection.
- Binding-on-seller's-heirs clause.

The contract should specify all restrictions and easements on the land, such as height restrictions, zoning uses, and utility easements.

Also have the seller list all known defects in the house, and if possible, all repairs over $100 made in the past three to five years.

"We had several conditions in the contract about cleaning and fixing up. These included:

- *Get the porch finished with carpentry and painting. (The seller did that.)*
- *Remove the above-ground swimming pool. (He removed it but did not level the ground.)*
- *Paint the fence. (He did that.)*
- *Remove the junk from under the crawl space. (The seller wouldn't do it, but we didn't cancel the sale.)"*—S.Z.

What happens if a disaster strikes before the sale is completed?

You are protected by clauses in your contract on Risk of Loss (e.g., by fire, floods, or windstorms) and Eminent Domain (government purchase of property).

The contract below shows the format and key items in a sales contract. You may encounter shorter contracts and have to add items to protect or benefit your interests. Or you may see longer contracts, perhaps with potentially harmful items that you should delete or alter.

Sample Sales Contract

This Agreement, made this day of _____ , 19 _____ .

1. *Principals Between,* _____ herein called Seller, residing at _____ ; _____ herein called Buyer, residing at _____ .

2. *Property:* Seller agrees to sell to Buyer all lot with buildings and improvements at _____ .

3. *Zoning Classification:* _____

4. *Terms:* (a) Purchase Price $_____
    (b) Deposit: check _____ cash _____ note _____ $_____
    (c) Cash or Certified Check at settlement $_____
    (d) Settlement to be on or before _____ (date).
    (e) The following shall be apportioned pro-rata at settlement: taxes, rents, utilities fees.

5. *Mortgage Contingency:* This agreement is conditional on financing described herein.
    (a) Mortgage principal amount $_____ Type _____
        Minimum term _____ Max. Initial Interest Rate _____
        Terminal Date to obtain commitment _____
    (b) Buyer shall complete application within _____ days.
    (c) Seller will permit inspections of property by authorized people.

6. *Special Clauses:* _____
   _____
   _____

7. *Personality:* All existing plumbing, heating, air-conditioning and lighting systems, as well as all ranges, TV antennas, wall to wall carpet, screens, storm windows and doors, kitchen cabinets, trees and shrubbery are included, unless excepted in this Agreement. Additional items to be included: _____

DOCUMENTS OF SALE

8. *Title and Costs:*
   (a) Premises to be conveyed by special warranty deed. The title shall be good and marketable.
   (b) Buyer will pay: premiums for title insurance, title search, appraisal fees, and Buyer's normal settlement costs unless otherwise stated: _____
   (c) Any surveys required will be paid by Seller.
   (d) In the event Seller is unable to give good and marketable title, Buyer shall have the option of taking such title as Seller can give, or cancel the purchase and be repaid all monies paid to Seller.

9. *Payment of Deposit:* shall be made to agent for the Seller, who shall retain it until completion or termination of this Agreement.

10. *Possession and Tender:*
    (a) Possession is to be delivered by deed, keys, and physical possession of property at time of settlement, unless otherwise specified herein. _____
    (b) Buyer reserves the right to make a presettlement inspection of property.

11. *Risk of Loss:*
    (a) Seller shall maintain property in its present condition.
    (b) Seller shall bear all risk of loss from fire or other casualty until settlement.

12. *Assignment:* This Agreement shall be binding upon respective heirs of the parties. Buyer shall not transfer this Agreement to another buyer before settlement without written consent of Seller.

13. *Agreement:* There are no other terms, oral or otherwise, except as attached to this contract.

Approval by Buyer:
Buyer _____ Witness _____ Date _____
Buyer _____

Approval by Seller:
Seller _____ Witness _____ Date _____
Seller _____ Agent for Seller _____

Be sure these clauses are included. If something happens, you can then call the deal off without losing any money.

What contract terms should I be wary of?

There are several provisions that may look harmless in a list of legal jargon but could hurt you.

Items you should delete from the contract:

- Provisions that don't give you clear title to the property. (Make sure the words *"clear and marketable"* or *"good and marketable" title* are in the contract.)

- Statements freeing the agent of any knowledge of conditions of the property.

- Assertions that the seller's obligation to you for the condition of the house ends at closing.

Items you should consider modifying:

- Declarations that you, the buyer, pay all closing costs.

- "Time is of the essence" clauses that don't allow you to extend the closing date.

Are verbal promises considered part of the contract?

No. Verbal promises are not legally binding. Get all such promises written into the contract.

"One of the most important things I learned was to make sure you know what goes with the

DOCUMENTS OF SALE

house. We lost a stove and a storage shed because we didn't get it in writing."—D.G.

How do I change any terms I don't like?

Strike out wording you don't like and add wording favorable to you. Initial each change. If the contract gets too messy, have a new one typed up. The seller uses this same procedure if he makes changes.

Can I negotiate when I will move in?

Yes. You may encounter difficulty if the seller is bound to a certain moving date in purchasing another house. But if the seller is highly motivated to sell, he might time any move to suit you.

Can I renegotiate the contract later, if problems occur?

Yes, if the contract gives you that right.

Your protection comes from "contingency clauses" covering circumstances that allow you to withdraw from the agreement. Suppose you have specified certain inspections in the contract and you are not satisfied with the results. Then you can cancel the deal or renegotiate it, usually changing the selling price.

"Our lawyer saw some major problems with the first contract we received, and suggested some changes. These included changing the

two-deed arrangement, giving us more leeway in making up missed payments, and placing more restrictions on the seller's ability to foreclose. Without a lawyer, we would never have seen these problems."—J.H.

Can I back out over *any* problem that comes up?

No. That would violate the spirit of the agreement. The contingencies should be worded to cover *major* defects or problems. You should not be allowed to back out just because your inspector found a loose doorknob.

What contingencies should I write into the contract?

A few key contingencies should give you enough protection. Beware of overloading the contract with contingencies. They might turn the seller off.

Among the most important contingencies are the following:

- Building, radon, and pest inspections.
- An appraisal that is reasonably close to the purchase price.
- A survey that shows the yard's boundaries to be what you expected.
- A mortgage commitment for the loan amount and terms that you need.

- A clear title, and title insurance at a reasonable cost.

- Occupancy of the house by a certain date.

These are basic and should be in your contract. Then if you don't obtain the desired results, you can cancel the deal or renegotiate.

"The seller wanted no contingency clauses, no binders, no earnest money. Just a real commitment to buy the house. For this, he was willing to meet our price."—C.F.

Can the seller write in his own contingency clauses?

Yes. The following are three of the most common:

- A requirement that you obtain financing by a certain date, or the deal is off.

- The time period that the seller can occupy the house.

- A "liquidation damages" clause. If you refuse to complete the transaction, the seller keeps your earnest money to cover damages.

The number of contingencies can be as long as the lawyer's mind can stretch.

What happens if the seller doesn't agree to my terms?

You renegotiate or the deal is off.
First, consider whether the dispute violates your

needs list (for example, closing date). Second, check on whether you might have protection from state statutes anyway.

One buyer finally gave up his requirement of a sixty-day default period when his lawyer pointed out that he essentially had this protection under state statute. Discuss the disputed conditions with your agent or lawyer. They are experienced in striking satisfactory compromises.

"The seller said he would not remove the tree stumps, even though it was in our contract. He also would not regrade the ground around the sewer connection until after the closing, after the ground had settled. I agreed to his oral promise to regrade later (he never did). I decided not to make an issue out of the tree stump removal, since doing so would postpone the closing."—J.H.

Could I lose the deal by taking time to have a lawyer review the contract?

Yes. However, it is not likely unless there are other offers pending.

Before you begin house hunting, ask your lawyer how much notice he would need to review your contract. Tell him your deadline for buying a house.

Can my sales contract expire?

Yes, if you specify an expiration or closing date in the contract. However, the date can be extended by mutual agreement.

DOCUMENTS OF SALE

"On April tenth the contract was written up, stating that it would be valid until the end of June. Our agent said sixty to ninety days would be needed to get financing and other details taken care of. We were able to close in June."—B.C.

Who signs the contract?

You, your spouse (if you are married), the seller (and spouse if he is married), and witnesses to each of your signatures. The witnesses can be your agent, lawyer, an office clerk, or a friend.

What happens to the contract after both parties sign it?

You and the seller each get a copy. The original is held by the lawyer or agent who drafted it.

THE DEED

What is a deed?

The deed is a document that transfers ownership to you.

What type of deed is best?

You want a deed that grants you the most protection against future claims on your house.

The most common is the special warranty deed, in which the seller defends your title against claims that arose during his ownership.

The most comprehensive is the general warranty deed, in which the seller will defend *all* claims against your ownership, even those prior to his ownership.

The key is to get a "clear [or good] and marketable" deed, with those words written into the sales contract. This means that the deed is so free of encumbrances that there are no doubts you own the house.

Can I get a better deed than the seller has?

No. If the seller has a special warranty deed for example, he cannot give you a general warranty deed. He can only defend claims arising during his ownership. If, however, he does have a general warranty deed, he can pass it along to you.

What types of deeds should I avoid?

Three types of deeds convey a questionable amount of ownership to you. Avoid them.

- *Quitclaim deed.* This conveys only what the seller owns in the property, which may be no interest at all. It is the least desirable deed.

- *Bargain and sale deed.* With a covenant, it gives you a guarantee that the seller has not done anything that would reduce the deed's value. This deed is better than a quitclaim deed. You at least get a guarantee that the seller has not endangered the title while he owned it. However, the seller is not agreeing to defend your title against all claims, as in a warranty deed.

DOCUMENTS OF SALE

- *"Double deed" arrangement.* Occasionally used in for-sale-by-owner deals. The seller and buyer each have a deed to the property, hence joint ownership. This continues until you pay off the mortgage. If a claim arises against the seller, you could lose your "share" of the property.

How do I get the type of deed I want?

Have it written into your sales contract. The title search will verify the deed.

Are there other ways to protect my claim of ownership?

Yes, through title insurance and a survey of the property.

Should my lawyer review the deed?

Either your lawyer or a title company should review the *history* of the deed, by doing a title search.

Whose name goes on the deed?

Your name and, if you are married, your spouse's name.

"Since only I had signed the sales contract, the deed was in my name only. After the closing, we had to get the deed in my wife's name, too. It seemed sort of ludicrous to transfer the deed

141

from myself to Clair and me. However, it was necessary."—C.F.

What happens to the deed when I buy the house?

It is sent to the courthouse or city hall to be registered with the recorder of deeds. You will get it back within four weeks.

Can changes be made to the deed after the sale?

No.

What do I do if I lose my deed?

Get a copy from the county clerk or recorder of deeds. You need not possess the original. A copy is just as valid. When you sell the house, a new deed must be written anyway.

8

Financing the Sale

The traditional way to finance a house is through a home mortgage. There are other ways, of course. If you're rich, you can pay cash and forget the loan business. If you're poor or handy, you can trade your labor for a house, or part of it, by a process called "sweat equity." But for most, financing equals mortgage.

In this chapter, you take a short tour through the mortgage market. The emphasis is on getting the terms you need, and seeing the loan application through to a successful conclusion.

FINDING A MORTGAGE

What is a mortgage?

The mortgage is a loan secured by real property—your house. If you don't pay back the loan, you lose the house.

Where can I get a mortgage?

From most lending institutions—banks, savings and loan companies, credit unions, and mortgage companies.

"Our agent recommended Prudential. They have special financing for people being transferred. We could prove we had transferred, because of our mortgage in Delaware."—D.C.

How should I begin?

First, find out if the seller's mortgage is assumable. That is, can the seller turn his mortgage over to you? If so, you may get an interest rate well below today's market.

Second, find out which lender holds the mortgage on the house. Even if it's not assumable, your initial finance charges may be less if you stay with the same lender.

How can my agent help me select a mortgage?

He maintains a computer listing of all mortgages offered in your area, with terms currently available. The list is updated daily.

FINANCING THE SALE

Some banks are more aggressive in promoting loans for people of moderate means or those seeking inner-city housing. Ask your agent which lenders gear their loans to your needs. But don't let the agent decide for you.

"I wanted a fifteen-year loan. But our agent talked me out of it. She said that with our income, it might be hard to qualify for a fifteen-year loan. Therefore we applied for a thirty-year loan with GMAC."—W.D.

Does my agent have arrangements with particular lenders?

Yes, in that his agency encourages business with lenders who provide good service. But not in the sense of illegal "sweetheart deals," with kickbacks.

Your agent knows which lenders get loans approved quickly, and which are notoriously slow. If you are in a hurry, ask him for a lender who charges slightly higher interest but rapidly approves loans.

How do I detect a dishonest lender?

It's difficult. With all the federal regulations on lending, the dishonest lender has been squeezed out.

However, watch out for one practice that a few otherwise honest lenders still try: You agree to an interest rate good for the next sixty days. The lender drags his feet, and doesn't approve the loan within sixty days. The interest rate goes up 0.5 percent. You ask why there was a delay. The lender says, "The credit bureau took too long checking out your credit," or gives another excuse. You are stuck with the higher interest rate if you keep the loan.

There are other lending scams, but they are rare. If a lending arrangement doesn't seem quite right, call your Better Business Bureau or Bureau of Consumer Affairs before signing anything.

Is it easier to get a loan on a *new* house?

No. You qualify for the same amount, whether it's a new or used house.

SELECTING THE RIGHT MORTGAGE

Are there different types of mortgages?

Yes. The most common are the fixed-rate and adjustable-rate mortgages. Check these out before considering the less common breeds, such as balloon, graduated payment, and buy-down loans.

What is a fixed-rate mortgage?

A fixed-rate mortgage is one in which you make payments at the same rate of interest throughout the life of the loan. The monthly mortgage payment does not fluctuate.

What is an adjustable-rate mortgage?

An adjustable-rate mortgage (ARM) is one in which the interest rate fluctuates with market rates. Therefore, your monthly payments may rise or fall, subject

FINANCING THE SALE

to certain limits. These limits are called "caps." There is often a cap on how much your rate can rise or fall in a year (say, 2 percent), and for the length of the loan, (say, 6 percent). If you want an ARM, get one with these caps.

The Mortgage Trail

MORTGAGE YOU CAN AFFORD
(with 10% Down)

Gross Annual Income	8%	9%	Interest 10%	11%	12%
$ 20,000	52,000	48,000	45,000	42,000	39,000
25,000	65,000	60,000	56,000	52,000	49,000
30,000	78,000	72,000	67,000	63,000	59,000
40,000	105,000	97,000	90,000	84,000	78,000
50,000	131,000	121,000	113,000	105,000	98,000
75,000	197,000	182,000	169,000	157,000	147,000
100,000	262,000	242,000	226,000	210,000	197,000

YOUR MONTHLY PAYMENTS
(Multiply figure below by size of your loan in 1,000s)

Length of Loan (years)	8%	9%	10%	11%	12%
10	12.14	12.67	13.22	13.78	14.35
15	9.56	10.15	10.75	11.37	12.01
20	8.37	9.00	9.65	10.33	11.02
25	7.72	8.40	9.09	9.81	10.54
30	7.34	8.05	8.78	9.53	10.29

For a 30-year loan of $100,000 at 10%:

100 x 8.78 = $878 per month
for 30 years

REMAINING PRINCIPAL BALANCE

After (years)		After (years)	
1	$99,400	15	$81,706
2	98,800	20	66,400
5	96,600	25	41,300
10	90,900	30	0

Should I get a fixed-rate or an adjustable-rate mortgage?

The choice is one of calculated risk. If you are a risk-taker, shoot for the potential savings of an ARM. If you have a more conservative approach to finances, you will have more peace of mind with a fixed-rate mortgage.

During the 1980s, holders of ARMs have paid out less interest than those with comparable fixed-rate mortgages. ARMs are becoming increasingly attractive. Lenders offer them at interest rates about 2 percent below those of fixed-rate mortgages. Many lenders offer the option of switching over to a fixed-rate mortgage at little or no refinancing charge during the first years of the ARM.

How do I compare mortgages from different lenders?

List all provisions of each proposal—amount, term, interest rate, fees, prepayment penalties (one-time charges for paying early on a mortgage), mortgage insurance requirements, and so on.

Add up the *immediate* costs to you: application fee, points, interest rate, and mortgage insurance requirements. The totals show which loan is the cheapest for you now.

Figuring the *long-term* costs is more difficult. You can figure your total interest payments from an amortization table. However, the value of a "no-prepayment" penalty clause depends on how well you can predict the future. If you are going to be transferred in two years, prepayment penalties are very important (and damaging). On the other hand, if you expect to live in the house the rest of your life, such penalties mean little.

What is seller financing?

The seller holds your mortgage. You make monthly payments to him.

What are the advantages of seller financing?

You avoid loan application and origination fees, and don't have to get qualified.

What are the disadvantages?

There are fewer options on terms, with little chance for an adjustable-rate mortgage. Some sellers demand a large downpayment, so you won't skip out in a few months. However, as your income rises, you can refinance with a conventional lending institution, selecting more favorable terms.

"We agreed on the price, but expressed reservations about the large down payment, interest rate, and length of the mortgage. The seller said he might be flexible, and asked what terms we wanted. He caught us unprepared. By the time we offered our own terms, his position had hardened. We should have been ready with terms right when we talked price, since he was willing to finance."—C.A.

Can I ask about seller financing, even though the multilist states "conventional financing"?

Yes, especially if the seller has paid off his mortgage. He might finance part (or even all) of your mortgage.

If the seller still owes on his mortgage, don't ask him to finance the works. Just write a small second mortgage held by the seller into your sales contract.

Most sellers prefer not to act as lenders. However, there are two types of sellers worth asking:

- Those anxious, even desperate, to sell in a hurry.

- Those with houses that won't meet building codes, and who want to avoid building inspections by lenders.

What is government financing?

Government financing means that loans are insured by the federal, state, or local government. Since the government guarantees repayment, the lender can make larger loans to you, with lower down payments and interest rates.

The most active governmental insurers are the Federal Housing Administration (FHA), Veterans Administration (VA), and Farmers Home Administration (FmHA).

How do I qualify for government financing?

You may qualify if you are any one of the following:

- First-time home buyer
- Veteran
- Low-income household
- Farmer
- Buying in a rural or inner-city area

Your agent or loan officer can tell you whether or not you qualify.

Where do I apply for government financing?

At a traditional lending institution, not at a government office. The private lender issues the mortgage to you.

"As first-time home buyers, we wanted an FHA loan. Our agent led us to an FHA lending institution. She even accompanied us on the interview."—S.Z.

When is my first mortgage payment due?

Usually the first of the month, with at least one full month elapsed since the closing. For example, if you close on December 22 or January 1, your first payment is due February 1. A few lenders require the first payment exactly one month after closing. If you close on December 22, your first payment is due January 22.

Can I pay off my mortgage ahead of schedule?

Yes. Be sure the mortgage allows you to apply extra payments to the principal first—not to the interest.

If you inherit a fortune, you can pay off the entire mortgage immediately, or you can occasionally make extra payments, paying your debt off a number of years ahead of schedule.

"I wrote to GMAC about paying off my thirty-year loan in fifteen years. They sent us a list of the monthly payments needed to amortize in fifteen years. In the GMAC payment book, I specify the amount to go to principal on the payment stub."—W.D.

"We got a thirty-year adjustable mortgage. The savings and loan told me that I could make

extra payments on the principal—that it was standard practice, and allowed in the mortgage wording. Basic payments are $225 a month. I pay about $250 to $275."—P.M.

Can I change the terms of my mortgage at some future date?

Yes, by refinancing. For a fee, you can change the interest rate, length, and sometimes even the type (fixed-rate or ARM). If interest rates drop 2 percent or more, you may save by refinancing to the lower rate.

How much will it cost to refinance?

The cost ranges from 3 percent to 6 percent of the loan.

To figure out whether the mortgage is worth refinancing, consider how long it will take to recoup the refinancing charge with lower monthly payments. If you can recoup the whole amount before you move out of the house, you should refinance.

Can I change lenders at some future date?

Yes. You can even switch from seller financing to conventional financing.

What happens if I can't meet my payments?

Usually, you have a grace period of thirty to sixty days in which to catch up. If you don't catch up, the lender may charge you an interest penalty, or declare the entire mortgage in default.

If you are in default, the lender will foreclose and put your house up for sale. However, you still have until just before the sale to catch up on your payments. If you do, you're still the owner, and the sale is cancelled. If you don't, the house is sold.

Yet you still have the "right of redemption." That is, if you make up the payments within a certain period, say, six months to a year after the sale, the title returns to you.

How can I avoid default and foreclosure?

Call your lender before the payment is due. He might be willing to work out one of the following solutions:

- Suspend all payments for a certain period (with a penalty added for the late payments when they do come in).

- Reduce payments for a while (with penalty added).

- Rework the mortgage for a longer term (for example, from fifteen to thirty years) with resulting lower payments.

Under what other circumstances might I face foreclosure?

There are several. They include:

- Failing to pay real estate taxes.

FINANCING THE SALE

- Neglecting to pay water bills.
- Failing to pay home insurance premiums, in rare cases.

Call the appropriate agency before getting behind in payments. Perhaps a solution can be worked out.

THE DOWN PAYMENT

What is a down payment?

A down payment is your initial payment on the house. Your down payment plus your mortgage equals the purchase price.

When do I make the down payment?

Usually at the closing. However, in a tight housing market, your earnest money (given when you sign the sales contract) may be your down payment.

How do I make it?

With a cashier's or certified check. A few lenders accept personal checks.

How much down payment will be required?

It depends on your lender.

A commercial lender requires a certain percentage of the purchase price or appraised value, whichever is lower. The amount can be as low as 3 percent with some government-backed loans, or as high as 20 percent on strictly commercial loans. The average is about 10 percent. However, if the seller is to hold your mortgage, the down payment is negotiable.

Can I borrow money from a friend or relative for a down payment?

Yes. Some lenders let you borrow only from blood relatives; others, from anyone. The lender prefers to view that loan to you as a "gift." He asks you to fill out a gift letter, declaring that the loan is really a gift.

"I needed the money for the down payment quickly from my parents, who lived over 1,000 miles away. Western Union was $150 for almost instantaneous transfer; and Federal Express, about $24 for door-to-door delivery of a large sum of money. But we chose a bank-to-bank transfer, which took less than twenty-four hours and cost only $14."—J.H.

Should I make more than the minimum down payment?

It depends on your finances. The bigger your down payment, the safer you look to the lender. Some lenders give a slightly lower interest rate with a large down payment.

If you have a lot of cash on hand, you can reduce your monthly payments with a large down payment. However, if you have little cash and savings, make the bare-minimum down payment. You need money for closing costs (about five percent of purchase price), plus a cushion for maintenance of your new home.

FINANCING THE SALE

Sample Gift Letter

I, _____ the _____
         (donor)   (relationship)

of _____ do hereby give the pur-
         (purchaser)

chaser, prior to the closing of the proposed mortgage loan,

$_____ as a gift, with no obligation to repay me.

Signed: _____   Date: _____
                (donor)

* *

(completed by depository of donor)

I certify that there are sufficient funds in the Donor's account at _____ to cover the gift above.
                                    (bank)

Signed: _____, title _____, date _____.

Construct a table with various down payments and terms, given your interest rate. It should look something like this:

PURCHASE PRICE—$100,000
INTEREST RATE—10%

Down Payment:	$5,000	$10,000	$20,000
Mortgage:	$95,000	90,000	80,000
Term: 15 years	1021	968	860
30 years	834	790	702

Monthly Payments

Pick out a combination of down payment and monthly payments that suits your pocketbook.

"I wanted to keep my payments below $400. Therefore I cashed in $25,000 worth of stocks, and used it as the down payment. That left a mortgage of only $40,000, with monthly payments under $400. I figured that when I sold my old house, I could use the proceeds to buy back the stock."—W.H.

Can I pay less than the required minimum down payment?

No. You can negotiate interest rates and points to a degree, but not the minimum down.

APPLYING FOR THE MORTGAGE LOAN

How should I get ready?

First, clean up or at least reduce your debts, if you have any. Second, gather up supporting material to go with the application: your sales contract; a set of building plans and specifications (for a new house); if self-employed, your recent business statements.

"Before making the loan application, we doubled the payments on our auto. We paid up all our credit debts. Then we reported a clean slate on the application."—W.D.

FINANCING THE SALE

How do I apply for a mortgage?

Ask the lending institution for an application. Get it filled out before going to the loan interview. This way the loan officer can review the application for completeness, fill in any blanks, and begin the review process.

What is on the application?

All information about your financial situation: employers and pay, credit cards, checking and savings accounts, other investments, and property assets, such as cars, homes, and yachts. Finally, your signature.

Signing the application does *not* bind you to accept the loan if it is approved.

"Since we are both free-lancers, it was hard getting a mortgage approved. The banks were nervous about our fluctuating income."—C.C.

Should I apply at more than one place?

No. Before you apply anywhere, you should know which lender has the best mortgage for you, and whether you qualify. Additional applications are a waste of money.

"We first wanted to apply everywhere. But because the application fees were so high and the interviews so grueling, we didn't."—C.C.

How does a lender charge me?

In three ways:

- An application fee for reviewing your request (about $150 to $300).
- Interest on the loan for its duration.
- An initial charge, called "points," for giving you the loan (usually 1 to 4 percent of loan value). One point equals 1 percent of the loan.

With so many competing lenders, some now offer loans with no points.

Your application fee should be about the same, regardless of the size or type of loan. For expensive houses, you may pay slightly more, perhaps $25 to $50 extra. The fee is not refundable, even if you are turned down.

"We wanted to avoid a premature loan processing fee of $200. After the sale was firm, we filled out the application forms. However, we told the bank to hold up processing until the house passed inspection."—E.F.

Should my agent attend the meeting with me?

Yes, definitely. The agent will make sure you bring the required information, and will find out exactly what's needed to get the approval. Many buyers find that having the agent along makes for a more relaxed interview. He is someone they can turn to if a difficult question arises.

FINANCING THE SALE

What should I keep in mind?

Know your rights. Until a few years ago, some lenders refused to count the wife's income. Today, under the Equal Credit Opportunity Act, they must do so. The lender is also forbidden to ask whether a woman plans to continue working or to have children.

Also, remember your deadlines. Let the loan officer know if closing the deal depends on getting the loan by a certain date.

"For Prudential, I just called a toll-free 800 number. The phone interview took about half an hour. The interviewer asked for the names of our bank, credit cards, our salaries, and where we worked. This was followed by a written application, where we supplied copies of our last two bank statements and last pay slip."
—D.C.

Can I negotiate the terms of the mortgage?

Yes, if you are a long-time customer or have substantial investments with the lender. For example, ask for a reduction in interest rate (up to 1 percent), or in points (one or two), or for a five-year extension of the loan.

There are some terms a lender won't give you unless you ask. After you find two or three lenders that look good, go back and ask for the following (if not already granted):

- A "prepayment clause" allowing you to make

extra payments on principal without an interest penalty.

- An assumable mortgage, allowing future buyers to assume your mortgage rather than refinance.
- A guaranteed interest rate in writing from the date of application, not the date of approval.
- A guarantee that if the interest rate goes down during the loan review, you will get the lower rate.

Some lenders also give you certain choices not really in the realm of negotiation; for example, you could choose between reduced points or reduced interest rate. And you can often select, or "lock in," the interest rate you want between loan approval and the closing. If these choices are not offered, ask for them.

"I wanted a mortgage that would start showing some equity after a couple of years. Based on amortization tables, I came up with a proposal for the bank: $55,000 loan, 10¼ percent fixed-rate, for twenty years.

"At first the bank rejected my proposal. They were pushing adjustable-rate mortgages. I protested that I had been doing business with the bank all my life. If they would not accept the proposal, I would take all my money elsewhere. The two bank officers talked it over, and granted me the loan."—J.W.

FINANCING THE SALE

"With Prudential, we could call every day on a toll-free number to check the interest rate. We took the rate offered ten days before settlement."—D.C.

"When I applied, the interest rate was 8.2 percent, with a 9 percent limit. I could break the agreement if the rate was over 9 percent at settlement. By the closing, it was 9.75 percent. I didn't break the agreement, because I felt the purchase and financing were still a good deal."—J.D.

"At the interview, the lender wanted ¼ point more than my agent's 'dump sheet' had shown. The agent didn't make a case of it. I was told by the lender there was no leeway, so I reluctantly agreed to the extra ¼ point. Now I understand that regional managers do have some leeway in rates. I could have pressed for the lower rate, or I could have walked out."—P.M.

What mortgage conditions should I watch out for?

Beware of the following:

- An acceleration clause allowing the lender, if you miss one payment, to declare your entire mortgage due and payable.

- A shrunken grace period. You want at least thirty days to make up a missed payment. One buyer was forced to accept a fifteen-day grace period, because the seller was also confined to fifteen days, an unfavorable chain reaction.

Even if you get stuck with these conditions, you still have protection by state statutes. However, if you delete them now, you won't need a lawyer to invoke statutory protection later.

PROCESSING THE LOAN

How does a lender process my application?

By verifying the information on your application form. The local credit bureau runs a check of your credit history. The lender may call your employers.

"Our loan officer seemed disorganized, and caused a delay in getting the loan. She didn't complete part of the application, misinterpreted our bank statement, and didn't get correct comparables in the appraisal. Fortunately, our agent attended the meeting, and called the loan officer periodically to check on progress."—S.S.

What is the first thing I should hear about my application?

Three days after you apply, the lender is required by federal law to send you an estimate of your closing costs.

FINANCING THE SALE

How long does it take to get a mortgage approved?

The average is about four to six weeks, with a range of from two to twelve weeks. It depends on how busy and efficient the lender is.

Can my agent and I speed up the loan approval?

Yes. At your interview, ask for the names and phone numbers of the appraiser, building inspector, surveyor, and credit-reporting firm providing information. This puts the lender on notice that you don't want any foot-dragging. If need be, you can call and push these people to get their jobs done on time.

Have your agent periodically call the lender to determine the status of the application. If the lender reports slow progress, your agent can remind him that his agency may look unfavorably on future business with the lender. This gentle nudge is especially effective if the agency does a lot of business with the lender.

Who draws up the mortgage?

A loan officer of the lending institution. (At the interview, ask who it will be.) It may or may not be the person who interviews you.

How am I notified that my loan is approved?

By a commitment letter from your lender.
The commitment states the terms of the loan, and

is good for a certain period, usually sixty to ninety days or longer. Even if interest rates go up during that period, your contract is good for the committed rate.

You have up to two weeks to accept the loan. If you do accept, you can still back out of it right up to the closing. (You lose your application and loan origination fees, of course.)

"When the loan was approved, we got a fat letter from the bank with all kinds of stuff. When we were rejected, we got a thin letter. You can tell whether you got the loan or not by the thickness of the envelope."—C.C.

Who should review my mortgage before I sign it?

Get your own lawyer to review it. Some lenders require you to do just that. If you don't have a lawyer, they will give you two or three names. Other lenders allow one of their own lawyers to review your mortgage. A lot of buyers choose the latter route, though it's not recommended.

What if I don't use the loan within the specified time?

You have to negotiate a new loan.

What happens if I'm rejected?

First, make sure you know why. Then find out what you need to do to get accepted for a loan. Go in person to see the loan officer.

FINANCING THE SALE

"After our loan rejection, we went to another bank, not to apply for a loan, just to get advice. The bank officer said to cut down on our debts, and 'look more normal.' We paid off the car and reduced our debt."—C.C.

Can I reapply for a mortgage right away?

Yes, either to a new lender or to your first one with some new terms, such as a larger down payment or a longer term.

THE APPRAISAL

What is an appraisal?

An appraisal is a method of determining the market value of a house.

A professional appraiser selects about three recently sold homes similar to the one you are buying. The average value of these "comparables" is used to determine what your home would sell for on the market.

"My appraisal comparisons fall into three categories:

- *Junk vs. junk*
- *Structurally sound (needs maintenance) vs. same*
- *Good all around vs. same*

Anything is resellable, even junk."—D.B., appraiser

When is the appraisal made?

While the lender is reviewing your loan application. Most lenders require an appraisal.

Should I get an appraisal before making an offer?

Not unless you have trouble arriving at a market value for the house. This might occur if the house is unique in the neighborhood, or if the inside is in terrible shape. Appraisers know how to figure market value in these cases.

Hire an appraiser before making an offer in these instances, but only if you have little buyer competition. Ask your potential lender to recommend someone. Either hire that appraiser, or find one in the Yellow Pages (make sure he has experience in residential appraising). This may save paying for a repeat appraisal during the loan review.

What do I ask the appraiser?

Ask about fees, procedures, and experience, as follows:

- Fees, both with and without photos of comparable homes. They run about $125 to $175 without photos, and $175 to $250 with photos.

- Home inspection and report. An appraiser should spend at least thirty minutes at your home, and two to four hours on the report. Don't accept a "drive-by" appraisal. Ask how many comparables will be used.

- Experience in residential appraisals. Ask whether he's done appraisals in your neighborhood.

- Membership in a recognized professional group, such as the American Institute of Real Estate Appraisers or the Society of Real Estate Appraisers.

Does the appraisal affect the purchase price?

No, not if you have already signed a sales contract.

What if the lender's appraisal is different from the purchase price?

If the appraised value is substantially lower, your loan will be reduced to reflect the appraised value.

If it's higher, you can celebrate. You've got a property worth more on the market than you are paying.

"I thought I had a bargain. So when the appraisal figure was about the same as the sales price, I was disappointed. But I learned from two recent sellers that appraisals tend to be conservative. They sold their homes for $3,000 and $6,000 above the market appraisal."—C.A.

Do I select the appraiser?

In most cases, no. The lender selects the appraiser, usually one he works with regularly.

What is the appraisal report?

It is a two-part report, with an estimate of the market value of your house.

The first part contains an evaluation of the house (plumbing, roofing, room size, and so on) and the neighborhood (growth, junk, land use). The second part has a list of comparable homes, usually three. For each, it gives the address, number and type of rooms, lot size, sale price and date, and an evaluation of condition. Exterior photos are included if requested.

You receive a copy of the report. Drive past the comparables to see how they stack up against your house.

"Prudential sent an appraiser out to check the house. The driveway and landscaping were not completed. Therefore they put $2,500 of the loan into escrow, not to be given to the builder until the work was finished."—D.C.

MORTGAGE INSURANCE

What is mortgage insurance?

Mortgage insurance is a form of life insurance that pays off your beneficiaries if you die before completing your mortgage payments. The purpose of most mortgage insurance is to protect the lender's investment.

With mortgage insurance, there are two types of beneficiaries: the lender, and your traditional beneficiary (spouse, dependents, partner). Some lenders require mortgage insurance, with the lender as beneficiary. For an additional premium, you can add your family or partner as a second beneficiary.

How does it pay off?

If you die, the mortgage insurer pays as follows:

- To your lender, a sum equal to the unpaid principal on your mortgage.
- To your other beneficiaries, a sum equal to the unpaid principal or the original value of the mortgage, depending on your coverage.

When is mortgage insurance required?

Some lenders or municipalities require it, especially if you have a low income or make a small down payment. With seller financing, the seller may pressure you to obtain it to protect him.

If it's not required, forget mortgage insurance that benefits the lender. Invest the several hundred dollars per year it costs in other ways. For example, you might consider buying mortgage life insurance (also called credit life insurance), which benefits your family. However, a long-term life insurance policy will do just as well.

"The lender, GMAC, required us to have mortgage insurance until the unpaid principal was down to 80 percent of the selling price. GMAC arranged for the insurance."—B.C.

Where do I obtain mortgage insurance?

From most life insurance agents and many lending institutions.

Can I get any amount of mortgage insurance?

No. Most mortgage insurance is for the full amount and length of the mortgage. If you want some protection in the event of death, but not a full mortgage insurance policy, buy a small term-life policy.

AMORTIZATION AND EQUITY

How much of my monthly mortgage payments goes to reducing principal?

At first, nearly all of your payments go to interest. On a thirty-year loan, you will reduce the balance on your loan very little during the first seven or eight years. You won't begin to pay more on principal than interest until about the twentieth year. This process is called amortization.

Where can I get the figures?

Ask your lender to provide an amortization table at the time your loan is approved. There should be no cost. If you are being seller-financed, ask your lawyer to obtain a table for you.

If you want the figures before making a loan application, buy a set of amortization tables at your local bookstore for about $5. Find the table that applies to you (size of loan, term, and interest rate) for the principal–interest breakdown.

What is equity?

Equity refers to your interest in the property above what you owe on it. At the closing, the down payment is your equity. As you pay off the mortgage, equity is the difference between your home's market value and your outstanding principal. When you sell the house, the equity is what goes into your pocket.

Can I use my equity *without* selling my house?

Yes. You can borrow on it, perhaps to finance home improvements. Lenders require you to reduce your debt a certain amount, usually to 80 percent of the total loan, before giving you an equity loan.

9

Safeguarding Your Investment

You have the house you want. Now, make sure there are no hidden bugs. Then put in some guarantees that it will remain a good home and investment well past the closing.

There are all sorts of people and things waiting to throw a monkey wrench into a good housing buy—everything from termites to tax collectors, radon to rainstorms. Protect yourself.

THE BUILDING INSPECTION

What is a building inspection?

It's an evaluation of conditions in and around the house. A building inspection should cover the following:

SAFEGUARDING YOUR INVESTMENT

- Plumbing
- Electrical system
- Heating and cooling systems
- Interior walls and ceilings
- Floors
- Foundation
- Roof
- Exterior walls
- Windows and doors
- Porches, garage, driveway, sidewalk
- Drainage
- Attic and basement

It is done by a professional inspector, and takes one to two hours.

What can I learn from the inspection?

A good inspection will reveal the following:

- Things not in good working order.
- Things that can be repaired rather than replaced.

It should also tell you (though you may have to ask):

- Remaining life of things in good order now.
- Improvements to help avoid problems or increase efficiency.
- Cost estimates of replacing items or fixing problems.
- Potential building code violations.

If possible, go with the inspector. A first-hand view of problems is far better than reading about them in an inspection report. A word of warning: Few building inspectors are experts in everything. Though the report may suggest replacing a furnace, have a furnace expert check it before taking action.

What is *not* covered by the inspection?

Most inspectors will not be able to provide accurate information on infestation by wood-boring pests or on the market value of the house. And though few are qualified to judge foundation strength, a good inspector should be able to advise you on whether a foundation "stress test" is needed.

"During my call, the inspector emphasized his experience as an electrician and roofing specialist. However, he said he was not qualified to judge foundations, something I definitely wanted to have checked. He said that only an engineering firm could fully judge a foundation, and their 'stress test' would cost about $350."—J.H.

Is a building inspection required?

Not necessarily. Your lender may require it, or just rely on an appraisal. Some older cities require one to make sure the house conforms to modern building codes.

Should I get a building inspection?

On a used house, yes.
On a new house, yes, unless you know the reputa-

tion of the builder to be spotless and the warranty to be comprehensive. Knock on neighbors' doors, and ask if they have any problems with the house or builder.

Who hires the building inspector?

The person or outfit that orders and pays for it. It may be you, your agent, the lender, the city, or the seller.

If the seller hires the inspector, can I trust the results?

If you ask the seller to foot the bill, he can hire whomever he likes. If you don't trust the results, your only recourse is to get another inspection, at your expense. Increasingly, the responsibility to obtain inspections is on the buyer. If given the option, you should hire the inspector and pay the bill.

How do I locate a good building inspector?

Ask your agent to recommend three inspectors, including their rates. If you're not working with an agent, call a mortgage officer, real estate appraiser, or your lawyer for recommendations. In the Yellow Pages, building inspectors are listed under Inspections—Real Estate or Building Inspection Services.

Anyone who wishes can advertise himself as a building inspector. When you call, screen carefully, asking the following questions:

- What are the inspector's background and

expertise? Is he just an electrician, for instance, with limited knowledge of other aspects of construction?

- Is he a member of the American Society of Home Inspectors? Members must pass an entrance exam and complete a certain number of home inspections before qualifying.
- What is his fee?
- What is the length and nature of the inspection? It should last at least an hour, and include even dirty areas such as attics and crawl spaces.
- What kind of report will you receive? Will he automatically include cost estimates for repairs and suggestions for preventive maintenance?

How much will the inspection cost?

The average cost is about $200, with a range of from $100 to $350, depending on the expertise of the inspector. Some inspectors also charge more for houses with more to inspect (for example, large or old homes).

Should I get an inspection *before* signing a sales contract?

You may, although it often takes one to four weeks to get an inspector. Your best bet is to write into your sales contract that the sale is subject to the house's passing a building inspection.

SAFEGUARDING YOUR INVESTMENT

What happens if the house doesn't pass a required inspection?

For those inspections required by a lender or municipality, any code violations must be fixed before the sale. If the problems are major, you may have to move the closing date back to allow time for repairs.

If *you* required the inspection as a condition of sale, you have two choices:

- Insist that the problems be corrected, or you will cancel the deal, or
- Try to negotiate a lower purchase price, and fix the problems yourself.

Buyers generally find that sellers prefer to fix up the worst problems and not reduce price. At best, they may agree to a limited price reduction. Be prepared to accept less than an optimum solution, if you want to complete the sale.

"After the inspection, we added up the cost of the three most critical repair jobs—new water heater, furnace, and electrical work. The conservative estimate totaled $5,800, the amount we asked the seller to reduce the price. He refused. However, he did put in a new water heater and fixed some of the electrical problems. So we didn't cancel the sale."—C.A.

What happens if the seller refutes something in the inspector's report?

Get his denial in writing. Attach it to the sales contract. It is evidence of your reliance on his word, if you should need to sue for fraud after the sale.

How likely is it that the inspection will uncover serious problems?

About 40 percent of all resale houses will have at least one *serious* defect, usually a structural or systems problem. The most common defects found by HouseMaster of America (55,000 inspections in 1984–86) are as follows:

- Plumbing
- Cooling and heating
- Roof
- Water penetration
- Kitchen appliances
- Electrical system
- Foundation

Most can be fixed, but the cost can be substantial. Among the top three, a new furnace can run $2,000 to $5,000; a new roof, $1,500 to $7,000; and new plumbing, $3,000 and up.

PEST INSPECTION

What is a pest inspection?

A pest inspection is an examination of the entire house for evidence of wood-boring insects: termites, carpenter ants, and beetles. Any of these insects can destroy wood.

A good inspector takes about thirty minutes, uses a wood pick to detect infestation, and pinpoints infested areas on a sketch map. He checks the following:

- Inside and outside foundations.
- Wood ceilings and floors on each level.

SAFEGUARDING YOUR INVESTMENT

- Wood beams where exposed.
- Attic, if house is over five years old, for evidence of powder post beetles.

What kinds of houses need a pest inspection?

All kinds, new and old. Wood-borers can infest wood quickly, even during construction.

Is a pest inspection required?

Some lenders require one; otherwise, it's up to you. If you want one, be sure to write into your contract that the sale is contingent upon a successful pest inspection.

Can I inspect for pests myself?

Only if you are an expert. Some wood infestation is beneath the surface, and cannot be seen.

There are certain things you can look for, however. The most obvious is little dirt tunnels going up the outside foundation. In the basement, look for evidence of wood damage where foundation meets wood ceiling and wood beams.

How do I locate a good pest inspector?

Ask your agent or loan officer for recommendations. Also, look in the Yellow Pages under Exterminators. Don't use the exterminator who is already serving the house if you want an impartial opinion.

How much will it cost?

About $50 on average, with a range of $35 to $100. The fee varies little with the size of the house.

"An agricultural extension agent suggested I get a free inspection from Terminix, since it was just as thorough as any paid one. But when I called Terminix, they said they don't issue certificates with free inspections, only with paid ones. Since my sales contract called for a certificate of inspection, I had to get a paid one."—J.H.

What do I get from the inspector?

If the house is free of wood-boring pests, you get a written guarantee to this effect. If not, you get a written report on the infestation, recommended treatment, and cost.

Can all infestations be treated?

Most can. The inspector will tell you if damage is beyond effective treatment. If it is, get a cost estimate of needed carpentry repairs.

Who pays for the inspection?

Usually the seller, but this is changing. To control the inspection, hire and pay the inspector yourself.

What happens if treatment is needed?

The seller pays for the cost of treatment for up to a year, assuming he agreed to the inspection as a condition of sale.

RADON TESTING

What is radon and how does it affect me?

Radon is a colorless, odorless, radioactive gas given off by uranium deposits underground. In areas with large deposits, radon may seep into the walls and basements of a house. Large amounts cause lung cancer.

How is radon measured?

In picocuries, a measure of radioactivity. The average U.S. home has one picocurie of radon per liter of air. The Environmental Protection Agency (EPA) puts the health risk standard at four picocuries. However, immediate action is not necessary until levels are much higher.

Do I need a radon test?

Call your state or local department of health or air quality for their recommendation. The EPA has found homes with unsafe readings in nearly every state.

How do I detect radon?

With a radon test kit containing monitoring canisters.

Some state and local health agencies provide free tests. Private companies, approved by the EPA, also offer kits and testing, usually for under $100. Contact your department of health or air quality for a list of these firms.

The most accurate testing is in the winter, when homes are closed up. But you can test at any time of year.

Who pays for the test?

For your own peace of mind, you should pay for and oversee the testing. Be sure to obtain a written report of test results, and recommended treatment, if any. Pay only after you get a satisfactory report.

How do I correct radon problems?

Most radon problems are correctable. Two correction methods are common:

- Sealing cracks in basement and foundation walls.
- Improving ventilation in affected areas.

Where a radon problem exists, the average cost of correction is about $1,000 to $1,500. However, it can be as little as $100 to $200 for sealing cracks, or as high as $30,000 to install a major ventilation system.

Who pays for correcting radon problems?

If readings are above a certain level, require the seller to pay part or all of the cost of correcting the problem. (For instance, seller pays all costs above $400 if the reading is over twenty picocuries.) If the cost of correction is above a certain amount, the sale can be cancelled. Write these stipulations into the sales contract.

"At our agent's recommendation, we had the house tested for three days. We got the results at settlement. The upstairs recorded a 9, which is fairly high. Since there was nothing in the contract on radon, there was nothing we could do. The report recommended retesting in the winter."—D.C.

HOME WARRANTIES

How am I protected against future defects to my house?

In four ways—building codes, court consumer protection decisions, seller disclosure laws, and home warranties.

For new homes, building codes offer protection against the use of faulty materials and workmanship. Likewise, consumer protection decisions give you an implied guarantee on the quality of new homes for up to a year, even where building codes are weak.

The disclosure laws (available in some states) are a relatively new legal tool to protect you. They require sellers and agents to fill out a disclosure form, spelling out all known defects of a property.

For a new house, your surest protection is a good home warranty. Some used homes also carry them, but most are of limited value.

What is a home warranty?

A home warranty is a guarantee that components of the house will work for a certain number of years into the future just as they do now. Any defects within that time will be corrected by the firm issuing the warranty.

Can I get a home warranty for any house?

You can for most new homes, though you may have to ask the builder for it. For used homes, warranties are not common, but can be purchased for almost any home in satisfactory condition.

"Not all of the builder's new homes were covered by a warranty. We got one because we asked for it in the sales contract. It covered all major and minor problems for one year."—D.C.

Who issues the warranties?

The largest issuer of new home warranties is the National Association of Home Builders, with the ten-year Home Owner's Warranty (HOW). The builder must be a member of the program to issue the HOW. Some builders prefer to issue their own warranties instead.

For used homes, several firms offer warranties. Some operate nationwide, such as American Home Shield; others, within a given region. They issue warranties for twelve to eighteen months, some without even inspecting the house. To find them, look in the Yellow Pages under Home Warranties.

You may find an occasional building inspection firm that issues warranties. More likely, the firm will just provide a report or certificate indicating the present condition of the house—not a warranty by any means.

What defects does a home warranty cover?

For new homes, warranties cover major structural problems such as shifting foundations and water seepage, and mechanical failures by utilities and major appliances. They do not always cover lesser defects like leaking windows and cracked sidewalks. But they should, and you should insist on it. Mechanical systems and appliances covered include electrical, plumbing, heating, and cooling systems; hot water heaters; and all appliances that come with the house.

Warranties for used homes generally cover defects in major mechanical systems (heating, cooling, electrical, and plumbing) due to normal wear and tear. In other words, if there is an inherent defect or if you abuse something, you are not covered.

Most warranties have deductibles. You pay the first $100 to $250 for a repair; the warranty-issuer, the rest. However, warranties for new homes should have *no* deductibles during the first year.

"The seller had reconnected a sewer line just before the closing. The sewer authority said it would not need to be inspected. However, we were concerned about its operating properly. Our lawyer suggested adding a provision to the contract, whereby the seller would warrant

***the sewer for one year. The seller agreed to this."*—C.A.**

Should I get a home warranty?

On a new home, yes.

For a used home, most of the time a warranty is a waste of money. However, if the house is over thirty years old and you suspect the furnace is about to go, or wiring is badly frayed, a warranty is a good purchase. Ask your building inspector or appraiser for his recommendation.

How should a new home warranty read?

Insist that the warranty be specific. Make sure you know the following:

- What materials, components, and appliances are covered? For how long?

- In case of defects, who does the repairs—manufacturer, supplier, or developer?

- Is there an arbitration procedure in case you and the builder disagree? (HOW has one.)

Finally, include a clause saying that the developer guarantees for one year from completion *everything* not otherwise stated in the warranty. It's unfair to ask that everything operate perfectly for ten years, but reasonable to expect it all to function properly for one year.

SAFEGUARDING YOUR INVESTMENT

How much does a warranty cost?

On a new home, it's often a part of the purchase price, at a rate of about $3 to $5 per $1,000 of house. That's about $300 to $500 for a $100,000 home.

Warranties on used houses sell for $300 to $400, regardless of the size or price.

Can I pass the warranty on to future buyers?

For the HOW warranty, yes. If your builder issues his own warranty, you will have to ask. For used homes, some warranties are assumable.

TITLE SEARCH AND INSURANCE

What is a title?

A title is the *right* to possess and use your house, free from the claims of others. That right is transferred to you by the deed.

How do I know my title is good?

By a title search. The search goes back through the records to the first owner of the house (if possible). It shows the transfer of title from one seller to the next. In some cases, it may even go back to the colonial period, when settlers were buying land from the federal government.

Is a title search required?

Yes. Normally, a lender will require one to protect his investment. He wants to make sure you own the place free and clear. (So do you, for that matter!) Always get a title search, even if you've known the seller all your life.

When should the title search be done?

Generally, the search is ordered by the lender during the processing of your loan. Don't request a search before the sales contract is signed.

Who does the title search?

Your lawyer or a title company designated by your lawyer or lender.

Since the records are public, theoretically, you could do the search yourself. However, this is risky if you are not an expert in contract law and legal terms.

Where do I find title search results?

On a report called the Abstract of Title (or similar name). It summarizes the history of your title in a couple of pages.

Why might a title not be clear?

Your seller may not have paid all his property taxes, or he might owe money to someone who worked on the property. These defects of title are not fatal, however, and can be cleared up.

SAFEGUARDING YOUR INVESTMENT

There are defects, though, that may nullify your deal. For example, if the wife of a former owner contends that the place was improperly sold without her signature, your seller may not have a marketable deed for you.

In most sales, however, you will find the title free of defects.

How can title defects be cleaned up?

In your sales contract, require that the title be free of all liens and other debts; in short, good and marketable.

If, during negotiations, you learn that the seller is fighting a claim, state in your contract that the seller will post bond guaranteeing payment of the claim should he lose.

If the seller has a lot of business debt, is the title transferable?

Yes, unless the house is part of the seller's business. But to be sure a lien against the title doesn't pop up at the last minute, have the courthouse records checked again just before closing.

"The seller had a lot of debts. At the closing, the seller's attorney showed financial evidence, indicating that the seller would pay his back taxes and general debt."—C.C.

"Our title search found nineteen liens and judgments against the seller's business. Actually they did not harm our transaction,

since the house was in both the husband's and wife's names.

"However, the bank's legal representative was afraid the creditors might crash our closing, and demand money. So the morning of the closing, he required my lawyer to check at the courthouse for any more liens. There were no more. But just to be safe, the deed was typed up in our names and recorded at the courthouse just before the closing."—R.K.

What is title insurance?

Title insurance is your guarantee that the title is really yours. For a one-time premium, the title insurance company will fight any future claims against you, guaranteeing that you keep the property.

However, there are a few claims against which you normally won't be protected. The most common is the unfiled mechanic's lien, an unpaid claim for work or materials that does not show up until after the closing. For a small additional premium, some title companies insure against these liens.

Do I need title insurance?

Yes. Your lender will probably require it anyway. Without it, you are unprotected if a claim comes up against your title.

How do I obtain title insurance?

If a title company does your title search, it generally provides insurance. If not, your agent, lender, or lawyer can obtain it for you.

When should I obtain it?

At least one week before the closing.

How much does it cost?

The cost varies with the price of the house, though not in exact proportions. Title search and insurance for an inexpensive home costs $200 to $500; for a $100,000 home, about $600 to $1,000.

HOMEOWNERS' INSURANCE

What is homeowners' insurance?

It's coverage that protects you against things more or less beyond your control, like fires and theft. It is sometimes called hazard or fire insurance.

Why do I need homeowners' insurance?

For three reasons:

- To obtain a mortgage.
- To protect against loss from fire and other hazards.
- To protect against lawsuits growing out of accidents on your property.

What types of homeowners' insurance are available?

There are two basic types: fire insurance and the package (or multiple hazards) policy.

Fire insurance covers only fires and a few other perils such as windstorms, hail, and explosions. It does not protect you adequately, and is not even issued by some insurers.

The package policy is your best bet. It covers not only fire and other hazards, but also the following:

- Living expenses in the event of severe damage.

- Personal liability and medical expenses for accidents on your property (to family, tenants, and all visitors).

- Loss of personal property by theft, fire, and other hazards.

You should have all of this protection. In fact, your lender will probably require it.

What is excluded from homeowners' coverage?

Floods, earthquakes, war, nuclear radiation, sewage backup, and water seepage.

You can obtain coverage for these exceptions, excluding war and radiation, by purchasing an expensive policy known as HO-5. However, it's not worth the cost unless you have some extremely valuable possessions in the house. Instead, obtain individual flood and earthquake policies if you live in high-risk areas.

When does my homeowners' coverage begin?

At midnight after the closing. The seller's insurance provides coverage until then.

How do I obtain homeowners' insurance?

Most insurance agents sell homeowners' insurance. First, ask the seller which agency currently insures the house. Call the agency and ask about the coverage and annual premium. Then call your own insurance agent, and ask about his coverage and premiums. Cost does vary among agencies, so check with more than one.

"My wife arranged for the homeowners' and flood insurance all by phone. We got it from USAA, which gives special rates to dependents of service people. We brought the insurance binders to settlement."—B.C.

How long does it take to prepare my homeowners' policy?

From a few minutes to a few days. Make sure you get it done before the closing.

If you select the agency currently handling the coverage, the agency can usually rewrite the policy in your name in minutes. With a new agency, it takes two or three days. The agency will take a picture of the house, but will not inspect the inside, unless the outside condition hints of bad conditions within.

How much does it cost?

For the package policies, roughly $2 to $3 per $1,000 coverage. For a $100,000 home, figure about $200 to $300 per year.

How much coverage do I need?

Make your overall property coverage 15 to 25 percent higher than your purchase price, because replacement costs (if the house burns down) will likely be higher. Adjust the coverage periodically as market values change.

Contents coverage is usually 50 percent of property coverage (and generally adequate); living expenses, if you're forced to evacuate, 20 percent. For liability coverage, the average is about $100,000, adequate for most lawsuits. However, for just a few dollars more, you can get up to $500,000 in coverage.

If you buy an older home that can't possibly be *replaced* at your purchase price because of unique workmanship and materials, ask your insurance agent about special homeowners' coverage for older homes.

Can I get coverage for theft in a high-crime area?

Not always. If you can't get it through normal policies, apply for federal or state crime insurance; this is also issued through private insurance agencies.

How can I get protection against flood damage?

With flood insurance, which protects against loss to your home and its contents resulting from a flood.

You can buy flood insurance from more than 200 private insurance companies in the U.S. The insurance is federally subsidized in communities that have adopted certain flood-control measures.

SAFEGUARDING YOUR INVESTMENT

Who needs flood insurance?

Those people in the 18,000 "flood hazard areas" in the U.S., designated by the Federal Emergency Management Agency. Ask your insurance agent, city engineer, or the Federal Emergency Management Agency (Washington, D.C.), if you suspect you are in a flood-prone area.

How much does flood insurance cost?

About $300 annually, on average. However, it can run over $2,000 in certain high-priced, high-risk areas like the Long Island shore.

Do I need earthquake insurance?

Not in most areas of the U.S. Seventy percent of the earthquake insurance in the country is sold in California. It costs $200 to $400 a year on a $100,000 frame house in California, and as little as $20 to $50 in areas where quakes are rare.

PROPERTY (AND OTHER) TAXES

What are my property taxes based on?

The appraisal of your property by your municipal or county assessor. The appraisal occurs once every so many years, at no charge to you.

How much can I expect to pay?

Between 0.5 and 3 percent of your property value, depending on where you live. If you buy an $80,000 house, figure on property taxes of between $400 and $2,500 annually, with an average of roughly $1,000. Call your local tax office for the rate in your area.

"The property taxes went up 50 percent after we bought the house. We should have called the governmental offices to check on them before buying the house."—D.G.

What happens if the seller has already paid the taxes?

If he paid them beyond your closing date, you reimburse him for those overpaid taxes at the closing.

Can I appeal the assessment on which my taxes are based?

Yes. First, call the tax office and find out the amount at which your house is assessed. If that assessment is considerably higher (say, 10 percent or more) than what you just paid, ask when you can appeal the assessment. In some localities, you can only appeal at certain times each year.

"After buying the house for $44,850, I learned that it was assessed at $57,900. The tax office said I could appeal, but had just missed the deadline. I would have to wait ten months. Meanwhile, I pay the higher taxes."—J.H.

SAFEGUARDING YOUR INVESTMENT

How will buying a house affect my federal income taxes?

If you itemize, and most homeowners do, you can take several deductions related to your purchase. These include:

- Mortgage interest on your monthly payments.
- Property taxes.
- Interest payments on related loans, including home improvements.
- Utility taxes.
- Energy saving tax credits.
- Certain closing costs, including points, prepaid interest, and property tax adjustments. Most other closing costs are not tax deductible.

With a mortgage of, for example, $50,000, the tax deductions will amount to several thousand dollars. Save all of your relevant receipts and cancelled checks. You will need them at tax time.

10

The Closing

Closing, or settlement, occurs when the seller turns over ownership of the house to you. The closing should go smoothly if you have followed the previous home-buying steps and have tied up the loose ends. Although others—your agent, lawyer, and mortgage officer—will be present, don't expect anyone to do the closing for you. The best advice is to be your own closing coordinator. Know what to expect.

PREPARING FOR CLOSING

How is the closing date established?

By agreement between you and the seller during contract negotiations.

THE CLOSING

Don't let an agent, lawyer, or lender dictate the closing date. Occasionally a buyer is pressured to set a date convenient for someone else. The date is what's best for you and the seller.

If the date is not negotiable because of your circumstances (new job, start of school), let the seller know this before submitting an offer. The date should be far enough away to allow you to obtain financing. A typical closing date is two to three months after the signing of the sales contract.

"After bantering it around with the developer, we set the closing for November 14th. I wanted time to sell my stocks, in order to make a big down payment. I even coordinated my vacation with the closing date."—W.H.

What happens if I can't meet the closing date?

Nothing, unless the sales contract specifies that "time is of the essence." In this case, you must settle on the closing date, or the deal is off.

Without a "time is of the essence" provision, all you and the seller need to do is close within a reasonable time of the original closing date. If this is too vague for you, specify in the contract how far back a new closing date will be (for instance, two weeks or one month). This is called a "modified time is of the essence" clause.

"The contract stipulated a closing on September 10th. However, we didn't have our financing

by then. The sellers gave us a verbal okay to extend the date. We finally settled on September 30th."—S.S.

Can I occupy a house before closing the deal?

Yes, if the seller agrees.

Let's assume that the seller is ready to move out a month before you have the funds to close. You can negotiate a clause in your contract setting the *rent* you will pay between the day you occupy the house and the day you close.

Can the seller stay in the house after the closing?

Yes. However, your contract should state the rent the seller will pay you. Make it at least market value, if not higher. You don't want the seller lingering past your occupancy date.

"One hitch developed during the closing. The agent had given us the impression that we could move in right after settlement. But she had given the sellers the impression that they could stay on two more weeks. After some arguing, we agreed to let the sellers stay, if they paid us two weeks' rent. The rent was half of a monthly mortgage payment."—D.G.

THE CLOSING

What happens if the seller can't move by the date I want to occupy the house?

Write an "upset date" in your contract. This is a date beyond which you can cancel the agreement and get your money back, if the house is not available for occupancy. This should only be a problem if, for example, the seller is building a new house, and is unsure when it will be completed.

How do I get ready for closing?

Review the closing costs and key documents at least one day before the closing.

You will receive a list of the exact closing costs from your lender at least a day before the closing, as required by federal law. Check these figures against the estimates you received when applying for the loan. In addition, review the following and bring them to the closing:

- Sales contract. Have all conditions been met by the seller?

- Mortgage. Are all conditions stated as agreed to by you and the lender?

- Inspection reports. Have all repairs been made and certificates issued?

- Abstract of title. Is the title clear?

- Binder or contract for homeowners' insurance.

203

How do I know the house is still in proper condition?

Do a "walk-through," as specified in your contract, the day on or before the closing.

Bring your sales contract along for reference. Is the seller leaving everything promised? Check for damage that may have occurred since you last saw the house. You should receive the place in broom-clean condition.

"In the contract, we added 'subject to a walk-through inspection the day before closing.' On that day, we checked all the utilities, and measured each room for furniture."—W.D.

How are the closing costs presented to me?

On a form called the Uniform Settlement Statement.

The Statement lists all of your closing costs on the left side, and all of the seller's on the right. The items on the Statement are grouped into categories. These include:

Sales contract figures

- Purchase price
- Down payment
- Deposits

Lender-related figures

- Payments in connection with the loan (e.g., loan origination fee).

THE CLOSING

- Items requiring advance payment (e.g., mortgage insurance premium).
- Reserve funds deposited with the lender (e.g., taxes).

Miscellaneous charges

- Charges for title services (e.g., search and insurance).
- Other settlement charges (e.g., pest inspections).
- Charges by the municipality (e.g., transfer taxes, deed recording).

The closing officer will go over these charges item by item with you and the seller at the closing.

CLOSING DAY

Where is the closing held?

It can be held anywhere. Often you will close in a conference room at the lending institution. In some areas, custom dictates that you, the buyer, choose the location, perhaps your lawyer's or agent's office.

Who directs the closing?

Again, local custom often dictates. Sometimes your lender designates a closing agent: lawyer, title company representative, or bank officer. At other times, the closing is directed by either the seller's or your lawyer or agent. Ask your agent or lawyer what is customary.

Who attends the closing?

You, your agent and lawyer (if you have one), the seller and his agent and lawyer, the loan officer, and perhaps a closing agent and notary. If the seller still owes on the house, his lender may also be there.

Actually, a closing can be held without either you or the seller present. In this case, you give someone else, a banker or title company, the power of attorney to close the deal. This is common in certain areas, such as California and Florida.

"The previous owner attended the settlement, since our seller still owed on the mortgage. We paid the lender, who then paid the seller and the previous owner."—B.C.

What happens at the closing?

There is no fixed agenda for a closing. However, it might go something like this:

The *closing agent* will:

- Read or summarize the contents of the sales contract and mortgage.
- Answer any questions you have about these documents.

The *lender's agent* will:

- Ask for your homeowners' policy or binder.
- List what you owe the seller (from the Uniform Settlement Statement).
- List what the seller owes you.

- Ask you to sign the mortgage note.
- Give you the money to pay the seller for the house.
- Collect the closing costs from you.
- See that the deed is recorded at the appropriate governmental office.

The *seller's agent* will:

- Ask you to sign the deed, which transfers title to you.
- Give you the keys to the house.

"As required by law, the lawyer asked the sellers if they were of sound mind, and whether there was any divorce or separation pending, when he filled out the transfer form. We all laughed, and that broke the tension."—C.A.

What if a disagreement develops?

Expect some pressure from an agent or the seller to close now, and resolve your questions later. Don't give in! Either work out a solution at the closing, or postpone the closing.

Buyers find that by tying up loose ends and going over papers before the closing, they avoid disagreements. The closing is *not* a forum for making decisions or settling disputes.

How long will the closing take?

About an hour, on the average. Some closings end

in thirty minutes; others last as long as three hours if problems develop.

What do I take away from the closing?

The keys to the house, copies of the sales contract, mortgage, prorated utility bills and tax receipts, and a copy of the deed. The deed itself is sent to the recorder of deeds, and returned to you in two to four weeks.

"At settlement, the sellers turned over only one set of keys. They never did find, or give us, the other set. We had to change all the locks."—S.Z.

"After the closing, the house would be unoccupied for nearly two months. We turned down the thermostats, pulled the water heater plug, and hired someone to mow the lawn. The seller's list of contacts helped us bridge this period."—W.D.

Exactly when does ownership transfer over to me?

At the moment the deed is signed over to you.

Index

Ad(s), classified
  house-wanted, 53
  how to use, 18–19, 20–21, 75
  sample of a, 21
Adjustable-rate mortgages (ARMs), 146–47, 148–49, 150
Affordability, determination of, 16–17
Agent(s), real estate
  attitude of, toward your lawyer, 110–11
  changing, 73, 85–86
  choosing a, 18, 55–56, 58–69
  closing and, 201, 205–7
  commission for, 24, 72, 106
  contract of sale and, 109, 129, 134
  cost of repairs and, 77
  deposit held by, 127
  duty, 61
  ethics and, 82–83, 134
  initial contact with, 63–64, 71–73
  lawyer representing, 28, 29
  listing, 59–60, 106, 120
  long-distance house hunting and, 55–56
  mortgages and, 67–68, 71, 144–45, 160, 165
  negotiating and, 64–65, 81–82, 104–5, 118
  personality of, 64–65, 85
  pressure tactics used by, 83–84
  purchase offer and, 103, 104–6, 108–9, 111–12, 113, 116, 118, 119, 120, 121, 124, 127
  as seller's representative, 29, 59
  specialties and, 60–61
  title insurance and, 192
  training of, 65–66
  visits to homes for sale and, 71–81, 88
  See also Brokers, real estate; Buyer's agent(s)
Allen, Robert, 44
American Bar Association, 29
American Home Shield, 186
Amortization, 172–73
Appraisal, 136
  assessor's, 197
  basic description of, 167
  buyer's, 102–3, 168–69
  cost of, 24, 168
  details of, 168–70
  lender's, 129, 168, 169
Assessment, tax, 197–98
Assumable mortgages, 144, 162

Backup offer, 54, 122
Bank. See Mortgage(s)
Bashinsky, Sloan, 112
Better Business Bureau, 146
Binder, 107, 123
  description of, 124–25
  earnest money with, 126–27
  See also Contract of sale; Purchase offer
Brokers, real estate, 66–7
  See also Agent(s), real estate
Building inspection, 102, 129, 130, 136, 151
  basic description of, 174–76
  cost of, 24, 178
  details of, 176–80
Bureau of Consumer Affairs, 146
Buyer's agent(s), 38
  choosing a, 41–43
  closing and, 40
  fees for, 41
  long-distance house hunting and, 41
  mortgages and, 40
  negotiating and, 39, 40
  services provided by, 39–40
  visits to homes for sale and, 39, 40

Classified ads. See Ad(s), classified
Clear (good) and marketable title, 130, 134, 137, 140, 190–92, 203
Closing, 193, 194
  agent and, 201, 205–7
  buyer's agent and, 40
  costs, 24, 130, 203, 204–5, 206, 207
  date and place of, 130, 134, 138, 161, 200–202, 205
  inspection on day of, 131, 204

lawyer and, 28, 32, 201, 205–6
  preparing for the, 200–204
  seller and, 200–208
  Uniform Settlement Statement, 204–5, 206
  what happens at the, 205–8
Commission, agent's, 24, 72, 106
Comparables file, 19–20, 101–2, 117
Competing offers, 119–22, 128
Connolly, William, 26
Contract of sale, 107, 114, 123, 190, 206, 208
  agent and, 109, 129, 134
  basic description of, 128–29
  details of, 129–31, 134–39, 178–79, 181, 191, 200–203
  familiarizing yourself with, 25
  lawyer and, 28, 32, 72, 109, 110, 129, 135–36, 138, 139
  negotiating and, 129, 135–36, 137–38, 200–203
  sample, 132–33
  seller and, 128–31, 134–39, 179, 200–203, 204
  for selling your home, 23–24
  See also Binder
Counteroffer, 114–17
Credit check, 22, 164

Deed, 130
  basic description of, 139–41
  details of, 141–42
  recording of, 24, 205, 207, 208
  seller and, 139–41

INDEX

signing of, 207, 208
Deposit (earnest money), 109, 126–27, 137, 155, 204
Down payment, 204
  basic description of, 155
  size of, 17, 150, 155–58
  sources of, 23, 156–58
Duty agent, 61

Earnest money (deposit), 109, 126–27, 137, 155, 204
Earthquake insurance, 194, 197
Emotion, house hunting and, 25–26
Environmental Protection Agency (EPA), 184
Equal Credit Opportunity Act, 161
Equity, 173
Ethics
  agents and, 82–83, 134
  NAR code of, 82

Farmers Home Administration (FmHA), 151
Federal Emergency Management Agency, 197
Federal Housing Administration (FHA), 151, 152
Federal National Mortgage Association, 48
Fees
  agent's commission, 24, 72, 106
  buyer's agent's, 41
  lawyer's, 30–31, 32
Financial statement, 109, 110
Financing. See Mortgage(s)
Fixed-rate mortgages, 146, 148–49

Flood insurance, 194, 196–97
Foreclosures, 47–49, 154–55
For sale by owner (FSBO), 45–47
Fraud, seller and, 96, 99

Good (clear) and marketable title, 130, 134, 137, 140, 190–92, 203
Government mortgages, 151–52

Homebuyers: Lambs to the Slaughter? 112
Homeowners' insurance, 203, 206
  basic description of, 193–94
  cost of, 24, 195, 196, 197
  details of, 194–97
  earthquake coverage, 194, 197
  flood coverage, 194, 196–97
  seller's, 194
Home Owner's Warranty (HOW), National Association of Home Builders, 186, 188, 189
House-wanted ads, 53

Income taxes, effect of buying a house on your federal, 199
Inspection(s), 135, 203
  building, 24, 102, 129, 130, 136, 151, 174–80
  day-of-closing, 131, 204
  lawyer and, 28
  pest, 24, 129, 130, 136
  radon, 24, 130, 136, 183–85
  seller and, 182–83
  See also Visits to homes for sale

211

Insurance
  earthquake, 194, 197
  flood, 194, 196–97
  homeowners', 24, 193–97, 203, 206
  mortgage, 24, 149, 170–72, 205
  seller's, 194
  title, 24, 32, 137, 141, 192–93, 205
Interest rates, 150, 151
  change in, during application processing, 145–46, 162–63, 166
  effect of, on monthly mortgage payments, 17, 146–49
  negotiability of, 161–62
  refinancing and, 153

Lawyer(s)
  agent's, 28, 29
  agent's attitude toward your, 110–11
  choosing a, 29–32
  closing and, 28, 32, 201, 205–6
  contract of sale and, 28, 32, 72, 109, 110, 129, 135–36, 138, 139
  deed and, 141
  fees for, 30–31, 32
  for sale by owner and, 47
  importance of, 27–28
  inspections and, 28
  lender's, 28
  mortgage and, 28, 166
  negotiating and, 28, 32
  purchase offer and, 28, 108–9, 110–11
  seller's, 28, 129, 205–6
  services provided by, 28, 30, 31–32
  title insurance and, 32, 192
  title search and, 32, 141, 190

working agreement with, 31–32
Leasing/renting, 53, 57
Lender. *See* Mortgage(s)
Listing agent, 59–60, 106, 120
Location, importance of, 37–38
Long-distance house hunting
  agent and, 55–56
  buyer's agent and, 41
  strategies for, 55–57

Martindale-Hubbell Law Directory, 29
Mortgage(s), 203, 206, 207, 208
  adjustable-rate (ARM), 146–47, 148–49, 150
  agent and, 67–68, 71, 144–45, 160, 165
  alternative financing, 23
  amortization, 172–73
  application fee, 24, 149, 160
  applying for a, 24, 149, 151–52, 158–64
  assumable, 144, 162
  buyer's agent and, 40
  choosing a, 21–22, 143–55
  conditional approval, 22, 24, 71, 109
  contingency clause in contract, 130, 136
  cost summary, 24
  credit check, 22, 164
  down payment, 17, 23, 150, 155–58, 204
  equity, 173
  fixed-rate, 146, 148–49
  foreclosures and, 154–55
  government, 151–52
  insurance, 24, 149, 170–72, 205
  interest rates, 17, 145–49, 150, 151, 153, 161–63, 166

INDEX

lawyer and, 28, 166
lender's appraisal for, 129, 168, 169
monthly payments, 16-17, 147-48, 152-54
origination fee (points), 24, 149, 160, 204
prepayment penalty, 149, 160-61
processing an application, 164-67, 190
qualifying for a, 21-23, 147-48, 149, 151, 159
recording of, 24
refinancing, 153
rejection of application, 166-67
from seller, 47, 149-51
Motivated seller, 43
  dealing with a, 45, 105, 150-51
  how to find a, 44-45
Multilist
  how to use, 19, 45, 49-50, 52, 53, 71, 72, 74, 88, 101, 150
  sample listing, 51
  what it is, 19

National Association of Home Builders, Home Owner's Warranty (HOW), 186, 188, 189
National Association of Realtors (NAR), 27, 43
  code of ethics, 82
  Realtor Institute, 65-66
Needs list, 16, 71, 138
Negotiating
  agent and, 64-65, 81-82, 104-5, 118
  buyer's agent and, 39, 40
  contract of sale and, 129, 135-36, 137-38, 200-203
  failure in, 127

lawyer and, 28, 32
no-nos, 118
rules of good, 112, 119
See also Purchase offer
Neighborhood, checking out the, 18, 38
  long distance, 55-57
New York Times Guide to Buying or Building a Home, 26

Offer. *See* Purchase offer
Oral purchase offer, 107, 114
Origination fee (points), 24, 149, 160, 204
Overpriced homes, 89-90
Owner. *See* For sale by owner; Seller(s)

Pest inspection, 129, 130, 136
  basic description of, 180-81
  cost of, 24, 182
  details of, 181-83
Points (origination fee), 24, 149, 160, 204
Prepayment penalty, 149, 160-61
Pressure tactics, agents and, 83-84
Price, home
  affordability, determination of, 16-17
  effect of seasons on, 36-37
  factors determining, 26-27
  looking above your price range, 53-54
  overpriced homes, 89-90
Property taxes, 197-98
Purchase offer
  agent and, 103, 104-6, 108-9, 111-12, 113, 116, 118, 119, 120, 121, 124, 127

213

backup, 54, 122
binder as, 107, 123–28
competing offers and, 119–22, 128
conditional on selling your present home, 24
counteroffer to, 114–17
delivering the, 111–22
deposit with, 109, 126–27, 137, 155, 204
foreclosures and, 48
how much to offer, 102–7, 110, 115–16
importance of, 100–101
lawyer and, 28, 108–9, 110–11
making the, 107–11
motivated seller and, 45, 105
oral, 107, 114
preparing for the, 101–7
seller and, 45, 105, 106, 107–8, 110, 111–22, 127–28

Radon inspection, 130, 136
  basic description of, 183
  cost of, 24, 184–85
  details of, 183–85
Real estate agents. *See* Agent(s), real estate; Brokers, real estate; Buyer's agent(s)
Realtor Institute, National Association of Realtors, 65–66
Recording of
  deed, 24, 205, 207, 208
  mortgage, 24
Refinancing, 153
Renting/leasing, 53, 57
Repairs and replacements
  agent and, 77
  cost of, 98, 180, 183, 184–85
  life expectancies of housing components, 97
  required, 179, 184–85

Sales contract. *See* Contract of sale
Seasons, home prices and, 36–37
Seller(s)
  agent as representative of, 29, 59
  closing and, 200–208
  contract of sale and, 128–131, 134–39, 179, 200–203, 204
  deed and, 139–41
  for sale by owner, 45–47
  fraud and, 96, 99
  inspections and, 182–83
  insurance of, 194
  lawyer representing, 28, 129, 205–6
  mortgage from, 47, 149–51
  motivated, 43–45, 105, 150
  purchase offer and, 45, 105, 106, 107–8, 110, 111–22, 127–28
  questions for, 78–80
  taxes and, 198
  title defects and, 190–91
  visits to homes for sale and, 76, 78–80
Selling your present home, 23–24
Settlement. *See* Closing
Survey of property, 24, 136, 141

Taxes
  assessment for, 197–98
  federal income, 199
  property, 197–98
  seller and, 198
  transfer, 24, 205
Termite inspection. *See* Pest inspection

INDEX

Testing. *See* Inspection(s)
Timing, importance of, 34–37, 71
Title
  basic description of, 189
  defects of, 190–92
  good (clear) and marketable, 130, 134, 137, 140, 190–92, 203
  insurance, 24, 32, 137, 141, 192–93, 205
  search, 24, 32, 141, 189–91, 193, 205
Transfer taxes, 24, 205

Uniform Settlement Statement, 204–5, 206

Value, home, 26–27
Veterans Administration (VA), 151
Visits to homes for sale, 87
  agent and, 71–81, 88
  buyer's agent and, 39, 40
  checklist for, 80–81
  costs of major repairs and replacements, 98, 180, 183, 184–85
  how many per day, 75
  how many per house, 80
  how much time per house, 88–89
  inspection list
    for a new house, 90–91
    remainder of house, 92–96
    top priorities, 89–92
    for a used house, 91–92
    worksheet for, 94–95
  life expectancies of housing components, 97
  seller and, 76, 78–80

Warranties, home, 185
  American Home Shield, 186
  basic description of, 186–87
  cost of, 24, 189
  details of, 187–88
  HOW, 186, 188, 189
Who's Who in Creative Real Estate, 43
Word-of-Mouth strategy, 52